BEN HOGAN'S
TIPS FOR
WEEKEND GOLFERS

BEN HOGAN'S
TIPS FOR
WEEKEND GOLFERS

SIMPLE ADVICE TO IMPROVE
YOUR GAME

TED HUNT

Skyhorse Publishing

Skyhorse Publishing books may be purchased in bulk at special discounts for sales promotion, corporate gifts, fund-raising, or educational purposes. Special editions can also be created to specifications. For details, contact the Special Sales Department, Skyhorse Publishing, 307 West 36th Street, 11th Floor, New York, NY 10018 or info@skyhorsepublishing.com.

Skyhorse® and Skyhorse Publishing® are registered trademarks of Skyhorse Publishing, Inc.®, a Delaware corporation.

Visit our website at www.skyhorsepublishing.com.

10 9 8 7 6 5 4 3 2 1

Library of Congress Cataloging-in-Publication Data is available on file.

ISBN: 978–1–62914–238–8

Printed in China

CONTENTS

Jim Langley with Ben Hogan at Cypress Point Club.

A DEDICATION TO JIM LANGLEY AND BEN HOGAN

The lasting rewards to be taken from this fascinating game we call golf are really the memories of those times spent with like-minded friends, and for many, there was no golfer more memorable for his thoughtful kindnesses than Jim Langley, head professional at the Cypress Point Club on California's exhilarating Monterey Peninsula.

Jim Langley   July 21, 1937–July 20, 2013

Ben Hogan was not known for his gregarious manner, but he was extremely loyal to friends and consistently generous to people who needed help. He was, despite a debilitating accident, the greatest golfer of his time.

Ben Hogan   August 13, 1912–July 25, 1997

Four friends on the first tee at Cypress Point anticipating their match.

PREFACE

In 2009, I wrote *Ben Hogan's Magical Device* for competitive golfers and professional golf instructors because none of them could agree on just exactly what "Hogan's secret" was. After years of caddying for, and playing with, some very special golfers, I realized that I had the long-sought answer. The only problem being that it was explained to me by Hogan's close friends in their undefined slang: "twist and arch," "wring the towel," "can't go left," etc. So, with help, I put such vague language into universally understood anatomical terms, and proudly gave a copy of the book to fellow Canadian Sean Foley for Tiger Woods at Augusta's practice range on the Tuesday warm-up session in April of 2011. This act may have broken several of the listed Augusta rules handed out at the gate, but Tiger had "returned" and was starting to look "very Hoganish." My hope was that Tiger would consider two special tips from Ben Hogan—the great champion whom Tiger was chasing—and make us both rich and famous. I was on cloud nine when on Sunday, five days later, Tiger carded a thirty-one on the outward nine to take the lead for what could be his fifth green jacket. But alas, he tore his Achilles tendon on a layer of shifting pine needles and finished in fourth place—not what he wanted. Recovery from an Achilles injury would take months, and the "Master's moment" was lost.

My second book, *Ben Hogan's Short Game Simplified*, was directed to those skilled amateur golfers who wanted to sharpen their game from one hundred and twenty yards and in, so there is a special focus on putting and chipping. Mike Weir took a copy at Shaughnessy Golf and Country Club during the Canadian Open in 2012 just after he had suffered a bone chip problem with his elbow.

At the 2012 Ladies' Canadian Open at Vancouver Club, Michelle Wie's father and coach asked for both of these books. With the interest shown by this trio of professionals, I thought that surely keen amateurs would be attracted by the fact that world-class competitive golfers used Hogan's techniques, and that amateurs would have a great time learning the secret to Hogan's power, accuracy, and reliability.

However, I could not have anticipated the difficulty of internalizing Hogan's swing system. It is so complex that it takes too long to be absorbed by someone who doesn't spend time on a golf course every day.

The average golfer, although keen to improve, simply does not have the time to redefine their swing. Tiger would take six months for a major swing change. Hogan asked the average golfer for just fifteen minutes per day for one week. But that disciplined investment appeared to be too much for the weekend golfer. The prescribed fifteen minutes was very easily preempted by demands of family and occupation. And so, after a couple of years of receiving feedback from golfers all over North America, and many lessons later, it became apparent that a quicker delivery of Ben Hogan's message was needed for the average club golfer.

This focus is what I have tried to offer in *Ben Hogan's Tips for Weekend Golfers*. The main technique instruction for these tips is designed to be put into action within minutes of reading. However, after absorbing the main structure of the tip—for those who have questions, in order to understand more of the swing technique just featured—I offer details to follow up on the presentation, so that readers can delve a bit more if they wish.

There are an amazing number of detailed facets within the golf swing, and it should be remembered that these parts are rarely separated from other actions. Therefore, ideally, further details should be considered immediately after applying the tip, because that follow-up process extends the likelihood of success, by explaining a question—so often overlooked in golf instruction because of time and cost—"why is this move so important?"

Ben Hogan's swing is as complex as a spider's web; the variables and connections are never ending. In this book, I've attempted to distill Hogan's system—quite usefully—to a selection of valuable but simple tips for the weekend golfer.

JULES ALEXANDER

The technique shown here is what separates Hogan's "power fade" from all other methods used for fading. His left shoulder is high, indicating a fade, and the shaft is pointing right down the target line. As you will see, his power fade is longer and more accurate.

INTRODUCTION

Golf, as you have no doubt discovered, is not an easy game—not easy for anyone. It's far too intricately elaborate, and let's face it, even if we were talking about your love life instead of golf, the game's complexity would give one pause. And yet, like love, golf is fascinating, and even though one can never get it quite right, it becomes the source of many discussions over happy memories and plans for future success.

Mark Twain spoke of golf as "a good walk spoiled." A succinct thought and quite possibly a true one. But it could be argued that Robin Williams has described golf better, and with more clarity, than any other man alive. He gave more detail than Twain when giving insight into the sport during his 2002 "Live on Broadway" show in New York. My thanks for sharing his singular performance as he presented a Scot's version of the invention of golf:

> *"Here's my idea for a f***ing sport. I knock a ball into a gopher hole."*
>
> *"You mean, like pool?"*

"No. F*** pool! Not with a straight stick, but with a little f***ed up stick. I whack a ball, it goes in a gopher hole."

"Oh you mean like croquet?"

"F*** croquet! I put the hole hundreds of yards away. Oh f*** yeah."

"You mean like a bowling alley?"

"F*** no! Not straight. Crooked, and I put s*** in the way. Like trees and bushes and high grass, so you can lose your f***ing ball and go whacking away with a f****ing tire iron. Whacking away, and each time you miss you feel like you'll have a stroke. F*** that's what we'll call it, a stroke. Cause each time you miss, you feel like you're gonna to f***ing die. Oh great, and here's the best part, oh f*** this is brilliant. Right near the end I'll put a small flat piece with a little flag—to give you f***ing hope. But then I'll put a little pool and a sand box to f*** with your ball again. Aye, you'll be there cracking your ass, whacking away in the sand."

"Oh, and you do this once a day?"

"F*** no! Eighteen f***ing times!"

"The Invention of Golf"
Written and Performed by Robin Williams.
From stand-up performance Live on Broadway
@2002 Carpe Iuris Consultos, Inc.
Used with Permission. All Rights Reserved.

With spicy dialogue like this, and masterful delivery, Williams shows us not the theoretical or the historically romantic side of the game, but the bare truth that has us all nodding our heads in agreement.

Ben Hogan's Tips for Weekend Golfers is designed to lessen the hefty load golf puts on conscientious men and women who work hard for the good life through their jobs, their children, their families, as well as for those who do not have the time to go into all the intricacies of Hogan's "system."

Hogan's system works, but it's too much for most. He was compulsive about the game. Some might say "desperate" given that he was born near the infamous Dust Bowl where he tried to eke out a living from golf. As a caddie he made sixty-five cents a bag. As a young professional his first PGA paycheck was $8.50, and then he took seven years before winning a tournament and $1,100, "the biggest pay-check of my life." There was this snarling hook that he had to change. So, when he realized this fact, he pursued that goal relentlessly until he stood alone, as the very best.

Most other folk have to be compulsive about their job—which, fortunately for most of us, is not playing golf professionally.

This book will try to arm the recreational golfer with good ammunition to fight through the complexity of the learning and ingraining process demanded by somewhere close to one hundred and eight variables. Thus they may avoid spending years in wonder, trying to find to find a consistent way into the "impact zone" with a fair chance of a solid hit.

We shall take some of Ben Hogan's observations concerned with the vital pillars of a competitive golf swing—one at a time—and present them as simply as possible. Following a few practice shots, which will help "re-program your old habits," the "Tip" should give you same-day improvement. For those with a little more time or interest, I will try to couch the quick-study, single-action tip into a context—or a story—and list some follow-up exercises and a few more details to give you a better chance to remember it.

PHOTO COURTESY OF MARINE DRIVE GC

Stan Leonard.

At this point I would like to emphasize that the following descriptions of Ben Hogan's swing thoughts are not from my own interaction with the great man himself. I got these descriptions and explanations from his fellow professional golfers, all of whom readily admitted that they were obsessed with discovering Hogan's "secret." I was fortunate enough to know three of Hogan's contemporaries. One was Stan Leonard—the head professional at Marine Drive Golf Club in Vancouver who, unbelievably, quit this plum-job at age forty to take his chances on the Gold Trail. He won three times on the PGA tour and had an enviable Master's record with four top-ten finishes. I was grateful to have played a lot of twilight summer golf with Mr. Leonard down at Point Grey, our neighborhood golf course.

George Knudson was another Hogan worshiper for whom I shagged balls at the CPGA tournament at Point Grey. I have always been amazed why, after he mastered Hogan's power fade swing so effectively, he did not take on Hogan's exceptionally successful putting technique. Jack Nicklaus said of Knudson, "A million dollar swing and a ten cent putting

George Knudson.

stroke." Hogan added, "You can copy my swing all you want, but leave my putting alone."

Moe Norman was an idiosyncratic golfing genius who was highly flattered that he was the only golfer whom Hogan ever watched practice for any length of time. In a sequence of lucky events, I got to caddie for Moe a few times when he came to Point Grey, so he got to know me in his shy way. Then one wonderful morning I was drawn to play with him in a BC Open pro-am at Uplands course near Victoria. The putts began falling for me during a miraculous spell of "in the zone" golf for a score on the outward nine of thirty-three. Moe, who was pleased for me, was nevertheless agitated at his thirty-four and repeated several times, "Amateur shouldn't beat a pro. Amateur shouldn't beat a pro." For the inward nine he proved his point with a twenty-nine and a tidy sixty-three.

After a quick dinner, the reclusive Moe Norman—called "Pipeline" for his unerring accuracy—went out alone onto the oversized Upland practice green and proceeded to fill each hole with a pyramid of balls. When I asked if I could pick up for him, he responded: "Sure. Good. That'd be good." When I had collected two bags and emptied them at his feet I took the chance of breaking into his shell of privacy, and asked: "Mr. Norman, how do you do that?"

Moe "Pipeline" Norman.

He pointed where he wanted me to stand. "Ben Hogan stood there...right there, watching me. He was the best. I copied him. Just a copy."

And then Moe showed me.

Along with George Knudson's zany explanation, I took both analyses to Stan Leonard who verified the observations of his colleagues. It was my job to take their slang terminology—"twist and arch," "wring the towel," "buckle the wrist"—and apply universal anatomical terms so that we knew what Hogan was doing at impact.

Autumnal Point Grey.

I've been very lucky for the time spent on the fringes of the golf world. My beginning was during World War Two. I was ten and there was nothing to do. My father was away for five years—with all the other fathers—so there was no Little League, no coaches, no teams. I made my way down Blenheim Street to Point Grey Golf Club and asked if I could caddie for the seventy-five-cent fee.

"Too young," I heard quickly enough, "Why don't you look for balls? They're worth money...no more rubber coming from south-east Asia."

So I waded the ditches, feeling with my bare toes for gold in the mud. And I learned where the golfers scattered the object of their efforts, and did moderately well financially, while trying to stay out of the way of tough looking, rough talking "rangers." And then a coincidence: a mare from the Southland horse-stable community threw her rider, and then found her way onto the course. Frantic, she galloped down the twelfth fairway and— "oh dear!"—across the green at least twice, with angry men chasing her, waving clubs until she came back my way. I picked a handful of dewy long grass and offered her a taste. She came over—nickering away her anxiety—and accepted my offering before letting me take the reins to lead her to the gate. The owner soon arrived just as Duncan Sutherland, the head professional from up in the highlands near Royal Dornoch, came over with a pat on my back and the offer of a job caddying. A new world opened up: the excitement of golf, the characters who played, and the beauty of the courses themselves...and they paid you to enjoy this new world.

I became a caddie for Mr. Sutherland, then a junior golfer, and later in life, with the security of a job as school teacher, a member of Point Grey Golf course, only ten minutes from downtown Vancouver, a city boasting year-round golf. Over the years I've played some wonderful courses—Pebble Beach, Cypress Point, Spyglass, St. Andrews, Monterey Peninsula GCC, Capilano—and I've played with some very interesting people: Sean Connery, Bob Hope, Michael Bonallack, Bing Crosby, Jimmy McLarnin.

So I have a few stories to use in illustration of various points. Some readers have found my stories difficult to accept…thought I was "putting them on" with dropped names. I'm not. As I said, I've been in the right spot at the right time, and I'm very grateful for these experiences both on and off the course.

The keenest golfer I know is Sean Connery with Hogan-like focus during competition, but completely relaxed when fishing.

TIP 1

AN EFFFECTIVE TAKE-AWAY

The Bing Crosby National Pro-Am was the most popular golf tournament in the world at one time. It first began in 1937 as a charity affair to help Depression-plagued local charities. Bing Crosby invited his Hollywood celebrity friends who were paired with golf professionals grateful for a relaxed way to earn some welcomed appearance money. The combination was a hit with both players and the galleries who swarmed to the three courses used: majestic Pebble Beach, the normally inaccessible Cypress Point, and the ultra-skill test-ing Spyglass Hill. The galleries laughed and applauded the antics and fun provided by ex-presidents, actors, and business icons. It was said to be one week in "Golfers' Heaven." There was nothing else like The Crosby, which continues today at the AT&T Pro-Am. As if a dream came true, and perhaps because I had caddied for Bing as a teen when he was on his way to a salmon fishing outing at Campbell River just a bit north from Vancouver, I was invited to play, and found that it really was all that they said it was.

The driving range at Pebble Beach was a nearby polo field rented for Crosby week. It served a golf purpose, even though it did not have all the amenities of an ordinary range. Therefore I was not surprised when I arrived with caddie at six o'clock a.m. trying to calm my nerves and warm up a dead cold driver. There was one other golfer waiting—Jack Nicklaus, who was not amused by the fact that there were no balls...so he sent both caddies to remedy this oversight. They left, and there I stood looking at the penetrating eyes of the best player on the planet.

I wanted to know if there was any one important thing that amateurs could do to improve their game, and I was surprised by the quick reply which was along the lines that it was an easy question, although the answer involved perhaps the most important move in the swing, and even though it was the easiest to do, hardly anyone did it right.

And so, to pass the time I suppose, here is what the great man showed me at six o'clock on a misty Monterey morning. Stan Leonard agreed with the description.

COURTESY OF KEN WEST

With characteristic tilt of his head, Nicklaus was steady over the ball and hands unchanging from the address position until time to hinge.

Set your hands in what you want the "impact" position to be. Squeeze the biceps to your rib cage. Then move the club head away from the ball by tilting down the tip of the left shoulder—the shoulder does NOT move toward the target line...just straight down the infield between the ball and your big toe. There is a new feeling to the hands. The palm of the left hand begins to turn skyward. The center of the right palm looks to the back of the ball.

The club face should feel as if it's closed, but it's really just square to the ball. The shoulder line stays parallel to the target line as the club's head moves away from the ball.

I don't wish to make too fine a point on this first position, but from past habit, it is likely that you usually start your swing with a hand-powered arc which pulls away from the target line.

After two or three hits, you might think that this take-away—which is new to you—"doesn't feel comfortable." I would like you to persevere. Comfort is not your goal. Shot accuracy is. Keep on.

When the left shoulder pushes the club's head away from the ball, nothing else moves—especially the hands and wrists. They feel and act as if they are wrapped in a plaster cast—a molded unit. The distance of about a foot away from the ball is comparable to the backswing for a twenty-foot putt. The hands have not swung inside the target line. This sounds different I'll bet, because you've probably been told that "everything moves together on the backswing." That action would be an easier move perhaps, but pulling the hands prematurely away from the target line in an arc demands a similar arc back to the ball, with a hope that it arrives every once in a while in the square position you chose at address. You can do better than that. Moe Norman thought so highly of the first stage of Hogan's take-away that he isolated it by starting the backswing with the club head twelve or more inches down the target line from the ball.

Even for longer shots the first phase of the backswing is the same as for a long putt, and the club face is moved away from the ball by the lead shoulder pressing back down the target line until the hands reach the right knee, still in "impact position." Then, for a longer shot, when the molded hands reach the right knee, the wrists will hinge for the move to the top of the backswing for a lob or a pitch. But please stay with the "first phase" of the take-away with putting drills. We'll get to the second stage soon enough.

Try this simple tip for your putting stroke, and watch your backswing start with a smooth and constant tempo. Later we'll put this simple, stabilizing move into the full swing...but learn it with putting practice, and watch the improvement over the next few days. We are influencing a large percentage of your game with this tip.

Grip for impact.

Lead shoulder pushes down.

The hands are molded as one unit, supported and powered by the triangle of the arms and shoulders. It is, of course, common practice that most players, for a take-away, pull the club head back from the ball with their hands...and primarily with their strong right hand. The club head is thus pulled back inside with such speed that control and correct timing for the rest of the swing is almost impossible, and in putting, deceleration back to the ball is an all-too-frequent result.

My apologies to all lefties. If you want to see the move your way—watch in a mirror and you will catch the action you should perform, and put that image into your collection of swing thoughts. Of course, don't forget that Ben Hogan began as a left hander who played from the right side, with his "power hand" out in front of the club head where it belongs. I have a friend who is right handed but putts left handed to get the stronger hand out front. And another aside: this square takeaway with the shoulder triangle works well with the lower left-hand grip. The Hogan take-away also produces good results with the long shafted chest putter. If you have one—and wonder how you're going to get along without it when the new rule comes into effect—try Hogan's take-away, because his connected triangle obviates the need for an "anchored" shaft.

If a golfer brings the club head back along the target line with his hands, there can begin any number of problems because everyone has heard—and may even believe—that the lead hand is the dominant hand, and the only hand to change during the full swing. The right hand gets into its impact position at address and stays that way throughout the swing, in a firm concave wrist angle called "dorsiflexion."

This is an important instruction for you to understand, and feel, in order to perform the "easiest but most important thing to do in the swing." The hands remain fixed within a molded unit. So, it is probably logical, and effective, that the golfer puts his "impact grip" on the club at address and gets the feeling that he will bring that handset back to the ball.

Probably the best place to learn the correct first stage is to ingrain it in your mind by focusing on the take-away with your putting stroke, because Hogan believed that every shot in the bag should begin this way: the hands during the take-away aren't anything more than a molded unit driven by the leading shoulder. Nothing else moves but the tilting shoulder—down for the take-away—then tilting "up" for the pull of the club face through the ball. Thus, he argued that the putt was also a miniature drive because that is how the golfer should begin a full shot—the first foot of the take-away is powered by the left shoulder, and like a putt, nothing moves below the waist. For shots longer than a putt, the hips don't turn against the braced right knee until the hands get to the rock steady right knee, and the wrists hinge for the lift to the top.

In his famous book *Five Lessons*, Hogan states clearly, "As you begin the backswing, you must restrict your hips from moving until the turning of the shoulders starts to pull the hips around."

Lead shoulder lifts for hit.

Hands have not changed.

Take-away for Chips

This description of the take-away where nothing moves but the left shoulder will also be surprising to those who have been encouraged to use a "forward press," which is supposed to help you get everything moving around. Although, it should be pointed out that the forward press creates a new tempo—usually too quick—in the part of the golf swing where nothing gets hit. This press is no more than a security blanket that you don't need. What does it do? Some say it gets your rhythm going. Instead, cut out this extra movement and get your rhythm going with a nice smooth tilt of the left shoulder, then see how much better your big muscles control the tempo than do hand movements. Watch Ernie Els sometime. Besides, with that gimmicky forward press, the club's face angle changes—only adding to unneeded movement. Instead, hover the club head and get rid of all the uncertainty. (More later on starting with the putter off the ground.)

Hogan's swing emphasized "a stable platform" from which the golfer turned into the ball with reliability and an arc which descended onto and through the ball consistently. He believed that unnecessary movement created problems that grew as the collection of parts moved. So, the shoulders, arms, and torso were all "connected."

The upper arms—mainly the inside of the biceps—squeeze the rib cage, and hands are a molded unit moved only by tilting down the left shoulder. A raising of the left shoulder brings the molded hands back through the ball, so the putt and short chip are really powered by the triangle of shoulder and arms connected to the torso. Control by the large muscle groups are far more reliable than a "wristy" putt using the hands.

Hogan called this connected structure "The Magical Device." PGA touring pros later called it "the triangle." And this triangle moves the club head through the ball—not the hands.

The first twelve inches of the take-away was nothing more than the left shoulder pushing the club's shaft down the target line, taking the hands to the right knee where they would start the "hinging" necessary for a longer shot than a putt or a short chip. But for the first few days, please learn the take-away through putting before moving on to chips.

Short chip, no swing change from the putting stroke.

The tilting triangle provides power, not the hands.

Look again at the stable simplicity of this no-moving-parts take-away. It can be made perfect simply by "hovering" the

The hands move as one molded unit pulling the handle past the ball.

club's head. This elevated position, which you have to use in bunker shots, gives you the all-important tempo for an unhurried swing so vital when holding the putter and the driver. If you really want to get the full benefit of the stable effects of a rewarding take-away, use the hovered club head and develop a takeaway with the calm tempo of an Ernie Els or a Ben Crenshaw. When you think about the years that Jack Nicklaus and Ben Hogan addressed each shot with the club's head raised, you must consider the possibility that they knew something that we don't.

Address with driver.

First stage—away with driver.

The trouble with *not* hovering the putter is that in anxiety situations, you lose the tempo needed to perform well. Further than that, breaking the inertia of a grounded club during take-away can change the line, and if chipping without the hover, the club's head can get caught by the rough and knocked-off line.

Putter flicking off line.

Putter pulling inside.

Putter square, as it should be.

Drill for Take-away

Putting practice will ingrain the take-away technique required for all shots—this is why golf instruction should begin with the putter:

Step 1. Nothing moves but the left shoulder (especially not the hands).
   2. The hands stay on the grip like a molded unit.
   3. The right elbow rests lightly near the right pelvic crest, thus turning the right forearm into a "fulcrum" which doesn't change length.
   4. Did I mention that nothing moves but the connected left shoulder?

By drilling with the putter and pitching wedge like this, you are really practicing the first stage for the driver, as well as every other shot. You will now start noticing how many touring pros use the hover, and the first move of the take-away that you have been using for your putting drills. The touring pros really don't need to practice hovering—until the nerves hit—because they practice so much. You don't practice as they do, so give yourself an advantage and hover the club—especially for the driver and putter.

Potential Problems

If you have one take-away for the putter and another take-away for the driver, you're heading for problems. So, try out this take-away. Don't be surprised if it's a little difficult to catch onto right away. Didn't everything you've done well in the past take time to learn?

The short chip might seem awkward at first, but when you get the hang of it, you'll be sinking a few, while most of the rest are "gimmies." More than likely the first few chips will be flubs because your computer is having trouble getting out of your old habit of hitting with the hands.

Put your hands in a strong mold by squeezing both palms as if trying to turn them toward the sky. Let the "dimples" of both elbows turn upward. Think of moving only the shoulder triangle and hitting the ball with the tip of your right shoulder tilting down on the back of the ball. Actually, you will come to realize that your shoulder does not "hit" the ball—as in suddenly "speeding up"—the tempo is about the same as the take-away: smooth and solid, because of connection. It takes time to realize that the triangle is best powered by the left shoulder, and this truth is best learned with a few days of putting. Can you give this idea twenty or thirty short putts and short chips five minutes a day for about a week?

While you work this out, at least use the shoulder-only take-away for both putting and driving, and hover the club head for a good beginning down the target line, with a nice "smooth" tempo—not a "slow" tempo, but a smooth one.

Special Drill (because this first action is so important)

If you can't seem to catch the feeling of *not* hitting with your hands but instead using the tilt of the triangle with a molded set of the hands, try this: for a day or two make short chips with "separated hands" while tilting your shoulders.

The left shoulder provides the power for the take-away. The right shoulder tip provides the line. Make sure your elbows are squeezing your sides.

The palm of the left hand hangs on to the grip firmly with the last three fingers as if wanting to twist the palm skyward. Do the same with the last two fingers of the right. Hover like that and you can feel Stan Leonard's reference to "wringing the towel."

When ready for the downswing into the ball—tilt the left shoulder upward toward your left ear. The club's *handle* will lead the club head through the ball. Keep the right elbow on the iliac crest and feel the solid shot.

Twist your left palm toward the sky to avoid a breakdown of the wrist.

Handle only swing with twist by left palm upward. Sometimes this works after a few repetitions to give you the feel that it is the shoulder-arm triangle that moves during the chip. The hands are just "hanging on."

Recommendations to Make This Technique Last

Sorry to throw so much at you with the first tip, but these suggestions will follow into almost every tip coming up.

Stroke twenty short putts (five feet) and twenty short chips (ten feet) with the proper take-away for seven days and see the tremendous positive influence of the connected triangle.

1. Twenty to thirty balls per day at a dime on the rug, or on a green to a tee. Not the cup please—we're trying to ingrain a concept here. Putting to a cup with three or four balls is not good training because, as you may have noticed, you miss around ninety percent of them, and that's not good for your confidence. Whereas, if just before you march to the first tee, you stroke three balls from six feet to a peg stuck into the practice green, you will have stimulated your stroke memories. This is called "drill."

2. You will be aware of the sweet spot, and you will come to the first green with confidence from these memories. When you want to "practice" putting, to test your stroke, tempo, and sight of line, arrange a competitive scene. Take one ball, find someone who wants to compete for a dollar or two and practice "game-rules" putting. This way you don't delude yourself and confuse your computer which has the memory of, "I'll get another chance." My buddy and I putt for one hundred dollars a hole—no one seems to pay up, but we keep track.

3. For variation during the drill, you can separate the two dimes (or two tees) by twenty feet and do another thirty balls.

4. Now try the same take-way and routine for ten-foot chips—from just off the green to just on.

5. If you get bored, remind yourself that this exercise improves 55 percent of your game. So if you shoot an 84, and you can manage a 10-percent improvement in 55 percent of your 84 shots, this technique will soon have you scoring in the seventies (if my math is correct). And it all begins with a Hogan-like take-away with the club in the hovering position.

PHOTO COURTESY OF MIKE LILLY

Stewart Cink in first stage of take-away.

TIP 2

A CHECKLIST TO PROFESSIONALIZE YOUR ALIGNMENT

Believe it or not, touring pros—as competitive as they are—help each other out with feedback on the driving range. This is one of the strange elements of golf; there is sportsmanship within a dog-eat-dog world. Although my father advised once: "Don't take advice from someone with a higher handicap than you."

Don't get me wrong, the PGA touring pros are not tinkering with changes in someone's swing. As you watch good players hitting balls after a round, they often ask someone they respect to "take a look." The good Samaritan primarily sizes up alignment to the target. If they do try to tinker with their loop's swing, caddies get very upset.

Vijay Singh collects a covey of onlookers and observers as he tries
hard to be his own coach, albeit with aides.

At the Greater Vancouver Open in August of 1996, the
PGA tour returned to the West Coast of Canada. Arnold
Palmer had helped design the Northview Ridge course and
the Canal Course, with the Ridge being chosen by the PGA
committee for the tournament. All the players were pleased
with the scenic course, and their wives were thrilled with the
off-course hospitality arranged for them. Tournament direc-
tors had shopping tours to Victoria on Vancouver Island,
trips to Whistler Village at the world's number one Ski resort,
and lunches after the gondola ride up Grouse Mountain

overlooking their hotels in downtown Vancouver. The atmosphere was full of good cheer.

The only unhappy person, that I could see, was Curtis Strange's caddie. Curtis was the U.S. Open winner in 1988, with a follow-up victory in 1989, and he had asked a journeyman rookie for a "look-see" but got more than he had bargained for.

The rookie, called "Professor" by caddies, got carried away and gave Strange a lesson lasting most of an hour, where he had Strange repeating the take-away for full shots by holding the shafts of two clubs to form a "tunnel" through which Strange's club would pass on the take-away from the ball to the hinge point and back.

The caddie was fuming: "Two U.S. Opens back to back; the Master's in '85; British Open in '88, and the PGA in '89."

"What's the Professor got? Two wins in Canada. Right now he's 143rd in driving accuracy, and 127th for putting. Then there's greens in regulation. Wow! Tied for 131st! And he's giving lessons to my man!"

Anyway, despite the odd unhappy experience, players are very interested in their set-up. It's key to their consistency, and it is so easy to slip out of position—a little at a time—until, without realizing it, you have a big problem.

What tour players are usually after is a picture of their alignment. And sometimes you see the caddie performing this function—especially on the LPGA tour on the putting green—but more about that later.

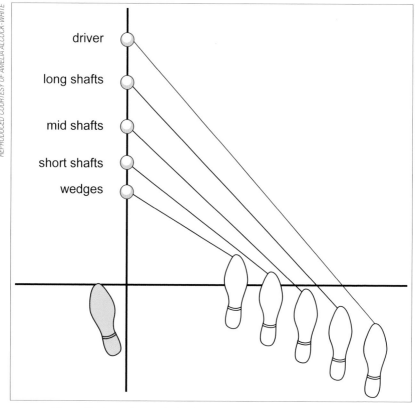

driver

long shafts

mid shafts

short shafts

wedges

Hogan liked consistency in his foot placement in relationship to the ball and the length of shaft.

Let's look at Hogan's view of alignment and how a proper set-up can help you.

Here's the way. You become like a pilot on an aircraft who completes a checklist before he takes off. Before each and every shot you play on the course, you have five check points. You will learn them, and they will become second nature to you. Running down your checklist will take a lot less time than a practice swing, which you don't really need anyway.

When another golfer is away and you are on the same latitude, looking at the golfer's back-side, he or she cannot see you. Do your fussing and stretching there.

When you step up to the ball it takes only seconds to go through your checklist:

Checklist: Learn This Procedure with Putting

1. Place your left foot on the spot you want it. It should be in that same place every time, and for every shot. Hogan put the ball opposite his left heel for every club because he believed that the brain would get used to that consistency, and the ball would be in the same place in the arc of the club face every time. Imagine the ball on a line to the target (target line) and set your foot accordingly, whether it be square to the target line, open, or closed.

Assign the left heel a constant placing for address. Your brain will thank you with consistent contact.

2. Check your grip.
3. Check your connection points at the same time.

The inside of the biceps are attached firmly to the rib cage. The right elbow is connected near the crest of your pelvis.

4. Hover the putter by flexing your posture muscles to pull the shoulder tips back.

Hover the putter for smooth tempo and constant line.

5. Now the important part: forget all the facts you've just checked out—1 through 4—and let the right side of the brain "take a photo" of the target. Glance down at the sweet spot on the blade of your putter and think of your photo image line to the hole. Now lower the left shoulder to tilt the triangle. Then raise the left shoulder to bring the club head to the back of the ball.

For the fifth check point try to "see" a pencil line drawn from the ball to the point of entry into the cup.

After getting automatic with this checklist, transfer it into your pre-shot routine for every club. You will have an "alignment process" for every shot in the bag. Think Hogan was exaggerating, and you don't need this? Well, Fred Couples didn't. Here he is with two of Hogan's suggestions—not only is he memorizing the target but he also hovers the club head— putting the odds for a successful shot in his favor. Couldn't you do that?

Fred Couples staring down his target line.

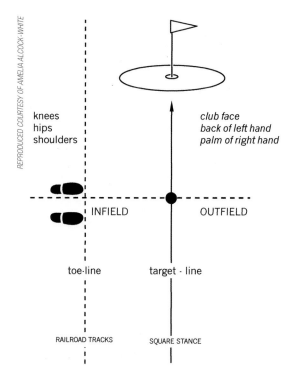

knees
hips
shoulders

club face
back of left hand
palm of right hand

INFIELD   OUTFIELD

toe·line   target · line

RAILROAD TRACKS   SQUARE STANCE

Square stance from "railroad tracks."

If you learn the memorized five alignment routines above, it is likely that you will not have to go to the trouble that takes up much of the day for Vijay Singh.

On the range at Spyglass for the Boy's and Girl's Club Pro-Am before the AT&T National Pro-Am. The challenge for Vijay was something like this: "Stay east of the angled shaft in the turf. East of the stick on the toe line, give the ball a smack, then stay west of the umbrella." You can do all this easier and quicker on every shot on the course if you just memorize, and make automatic, your five pre-hit positions before taking a picture of the ball's pathway to the target.

LONGER CHIPS AND PITCHES

Perhaps, after mastery of the first step of the take-away for putts and short chips, it would be useful to continue to the next phase of the swing, which requires two changes for longer shots such as pitches and lobs.

First change: The wrists hinge for the longer shot.

Second change: The stationary right knee moves—at last—under the ball down the "infield" section of grass between the target line and the toe line before impacting the ball.

Address for a long pitch with the right knee "kicked in" just a touch.

From the address position, the take-away begins as the left shoulder presses down toward the ball, and this action pushes the hovering club face back along the target line for a foot or so—to the point where the unmoving mold made by the hands reaches the golfer's right knee.

First stage of take-away for pitch. Hands still square to the target line.

It is at this point, at the end of the first phase, that the wrists begin to "hinge" as the hands keep moving down the target line—and both hands "cock"—bringing the arms and club shaft into an angle which for a full shot would reach ninety degrees. And when this angled hinge position has been achieved, you will notice that both hands have moved into a concave position called "dorsiflexion" with wrists concave and the palms facing each other. Note that the butt end of the grip is pointing to the "infield" grass between the golfer's target line and the toe line. Neither hand has "flopped over."

The hands are half way up to the top in dorsiflexion, with the shaft parallel to the target line.

The other key feature to note at this point is that the left side of the torso—led by the left knee moving in toward the centre of the stance—has now begun to move, by "turning in a barrel." As a result, the golfer's back should be almost facing the target—depending upon distance of course. Do this a few times in slow motion, because once at the half-way point, stop and you will notice a sample of the interlocking and interdependent nature of Hogan's swing system.

There are few side effects to Hogan's precise actions. If you look down the club shaft turned away from the target at the halfway point for a pitch or lob with a wedge—or perhaps a "punch" shot with an eight iron—you will notice that your club's shaft is parallel to the ground—which influences distance. But as well, it is also parallel to the target line—which influences "direction." Just another little detail designed to bring the all-important "repeating action" to the golf shot.

When the left shoulder rises straight up in toward the left ear, the right shoulder and the right knee turn under the ball through impact. And because the address position hasn't changed—as it would in a long shot—the "impact" position is in place. Therefore, the timing of the strike for this shot is "made simple"—the left hip rotates the right knee under the ball. At the same time, the left shoulder pulls the connected triangle through the ball. The top half and the bottom half of the body turn to impact at the same time.

There will be subtle adjustments to this timing later, for long shots.

The right knee rotates under the ball and the left shoulder rises. Again, you might imagine that the right shoulder hits the ball.

Just after impact, the belt buckle turns to the target and the shaft is parallel with the ground, pointing straight down the target line to the target. This position should mirror the position half way into the take-away.

The shaft pointing at the target on the follow-through is parallel to the target line. Hands are still in address mold.

The first touring professional to amaze me with his repetitive accuracy was Ted Kroll. He was a very calm man—a bit on the quiet side even. Perhaps this was because, like Hogan, he was very grateful to the "Gold Trail" for showing him a way out of the Great Depression. Also, he had survived his combat service with General Patton's Fifth Army and the ferocious 1943 invasion of Salerno, Italy, where he was awarded the Purple Heart for the wounds received during the ten days of fierce action. Now six years later he was making top money taking a walk in the park, and I was scheduled to caddy for him.

Kroll was fated to win eight PGA Tour events and would become the leading money winner in 1956 with a season's total of $72,836. He had won a close fourth place in the 1956 U.S. Open at Oak Hill in Rochester and would be runner-up the same year at Boston's Blue Hill Club for the PGA championship.

The shot from Kroll's play that stands out for me came during the BC Open at my home course. At the old eighth hole, he missed this small green to the right, leaving a twenty yard pitch over a trap to the old-style wooden pin which was as thick as a broom handle. He showed me how he wanted the flag stick to be held: firmly at the top and angled forty-five degrees down into the hole. "Don't move," he added.

His shot cleared the trap, hit the pin at its center, and then, like a trained mouse, ran down the pole into the cup. I was fifteen years old and too dumb to ask what he thought he was doing.

Thirty-three years later when he came to Vancouver in 1981 with the new Senior PGA Tour, he smiled when I asked him what he was thinking before that remarkable shot. "The gallery needed some action. There was a slope behind the flag, so if I'd missed the pin it would have pulled back to the cup. Hogan taught me that one. But you gotta practice."

Warm-up Drill Before You Play

1. Go to the far side of the range mat with your pitching wedge, and putt back at the rubber tee on the other side by hovering the straight leading edge of the club for a strike on the ball's equator. Take your molded grip and tilt your left shoulder for three putts.

2. Take the same club to the regular side of the mat and use the same putting stroke (except the leading edge now will strike well below the ball's equator). Chip over the long grass just off the mat, to a spot on the short grass beyond. On the fly they should travel just five or six feet—using exactly the same swing rhythm as for the putter. The molded hands are moved by the shoulder triangle. Imagine hitting the ball with your descending right shoulder.

3. After taking the half-swing described above, hit a few long pitch shots with a nice even tempo encouraged by hovering the club head, and make sure your right knee drives under the ball, just as the left shoulder rises up to the sky. When you have the timing smooth, and the contact crisp, move to the three quarter shot for a few repetitions.

4. If after 10 practice shots you aren't getting a good "click" and a good feeling on at least a few chips with the back of your right hand in a flat impact position at

address, try this adjustment—but only as a last resort to get you over this "hump."

Address the ball with your left hand in slight dorsiflexion. Then take a half-swing in slow motion. Turn your left hip to bring the triangle down and as your left hand goes past the ball, rotate the left wrist "flat" again for impact by arching your wrist and pressing your left thumb down at the ball. The right hand *must* remain in dorsiflexion through the entire shot.

5. Now bring the same timing and swing parts to the full shot—hit three or four. Quit on a good one...then go play.

PHOTO COURTESY OF JULES ALEXANDER

The left hip has pulled the right knee and hip into impact. Jules Alexander, the artist who took this photo, swears that Hogan played into the rough intentionally on the par five fifth hole at Winged Foot, because from this position he had an open angle to the pin and plenty of room to stop the ball.

TIP 4

ROLE OF THE RIGHT KNEE AS KEYSTONE

This tip is a game changer, and would likely have been Mr. Hogan's first choice to tell you. It's that important—and that effective. For long hitters who want or need more accuracy, this one's for you.

Ben Hogan was not overly gregarious with the public at large, but he did like caddies, having been one himself in the hard old days of the Depression. He had an easy rapport with these men.

Of course he was not without business-like demands, but he did get along very well with the "hired help" as "fellow sufferers," and often helped out these special members of the golf scene when they needed a hand with money.

Hogan's instructions to a caddie were often along the following lines: "Carry the bag. Give me the yardage when I ask for it. Don't ask questions. Don't touch the grip of the club, or the face of the club...I don't need skin oil, or sweat, between the club face and the ball. Stay out of my sight; stand directly in front or directly behind me during my shot. By the way, you'll be keeping the scorecard...I'll go over it when we've finished. I've got other things to think about right now."

PHOTO COURTESY OF GETTY IMAGES

Here's a burly caddie standing in the correct spot—although I can't imagine Hogan tolerating the location of the two officials in his vision to the right, and not directly behind him on the same latitude where they can't be seen.

But back to Hogan's point regarding the role of his right knee: In a more relaxed moment he said to his caddie, "Do you know why I'm so goddam good?" The caddie shook his head. "I never move my right knee until I'm in the impact zone."

And this is what he meant: At address, Hogan prepared a "solid" and stable foundation for his shot—in this case let's say a driver. His feet were ready to receive a balanced shift of weight from within a slightly "closed" position for his feet—the left foot was turned half-way from a perpendicular position to forty-five degrees, toward the target.

Today there are not too many touring pros who do not hover their driver.

Hogan's right foot was perpendicular to the target line with the right knee pressed in toward the center of the stance...just over the inside edge of his made-in-England $1,200 golf shoes. Seventy percent of his weight was set above the inside edge of the right shoe, and this weight is distributed between the base of the big toe (not the tip of the big toe) and the inside edge of the right heel. The "feeling" is as if you are on the "inside edge" of your hockey skates or your skis. The right knee is "kicked in" toward the center of the stance.

Correct hip rotation with knee kicked in.

As the left shoulder turns behind the ball, the right knee holds its position without any movement. The left knee turns in a little to form the "K" Sam Snead often spoke of.

The golfer's weight *never* shifts to the outside edge of the right shoe above the little toe. (I first learned this detail from Dick Zokol—another Hogan aficionado—at the Crosby National Pro-Am.)

Incorrect knee take-away. Weight on outside of right foot.

As soon as the downswing to the impact zone begins, the right knee "fires" down the "infield" under the ball and toward the target.

Right side driving under ball. Arms still strongly connected to the rib cage.

The right hip and the right shoulder follow under the ball and not "over the top" of the ball toward the "outfield." If the golfer's first move is with the tip of the right shoulder moving out over the ball toward the "outfield," it is usually accompanied by a "straightening of the leading leg and a terrible shot."

Incorrect move over the top. The lower body should lead the way on long shots—not the right hand and shoulder.

PHOTO COURTESY OF MIKE LILLY

Tiger's weight is "torqued" into the inside edge of his right foot. This rock solid position at the top is a textbook display for balance and stability.

In this photo (above), Tiger Woods provides a textbook example as his knees are moving together in a counter-clockwise rotation toward the target as he begins to settle into the bar-stool position. This action for long shots will turn the upper triangle into play after the lower half leads, and will thereby separate the bottom half of the body from the top half. For long shots there is a slightly different timing than lobs and pitches which are half shots—where both halves of the body can move at the same time because they started the impact position at address, with hips turned counter clockwise and the stance "open."

Perhaps Lindsey Vonn has emphasized this action with Tiger where the inside edge of his right ski is unmovable. With solid balance, Tiger will drive the right side of his body, down under his chin, under the ball, and under the highest point of the lead shoulder, and then on down the target line.

TIP 5

HALF-DECENT BUNKER SHOTS

Stan Leonard, a respected friend to Ben Hogan, won the Tournament of Champions at the Las Vegas National Golf Club in April 1958. He posted three scores of 69 and looked like he might shoot another, even though he buried his tee shot in a nasty green-side bunker on the 214-yard par three sixteenth hole while straining to finish well on the final day. Apparently there was no problem; he calmly sunk that bunker shot to post a tidy 68—good for a one-shot win over Billy Casper. The victory was his, with the first prize of a wheelbarrow holding 10,000 silver dollars. He took great care over sand shots from that day on.

A side-bar story to that win was interesting. A man approached Stan after the award ceremony and invited him up for a drink to celebrate. To cut a long story short: the host turned out to be Gordon MacRae, who was the male lead in the film of the musical *Oklahoma*, and who had bet big on Stan. Despite Stan's protestations, MacRae forced 10 percent of his Las Vegas winnings on the stunned Canadian, and Stan went home with $20,000 at a time when $2,000 was the usual winner's prize. Not bad for a forty-one-year-old club pro who had "rolled the dice" on whether he could make it on the PGA Tour.

I met Stan one day when he was on a fitness walk along Marine Drive not far from his Vancouver home.

"How's your game?" he asked.

"Not bad, pro...except for sand traps. Then it's screaming-in-hell bad."

"Maybe we should fix that," he said convincingly.

At the short game area the next morning, he began: "Hogan didn't get into too many traps. I'll show you how he handled them. Because oddly enough, amateurs can take their worst fault and make it their best weapon when they step into a bunker. It's a different world in there, you know."

What Leonard then explained was that, during a golf swing, it is the objective to never collapse the left wrist at impact...but amateurs do break down the leading wrist with alarming regularity, thus producing a wondrous array of bad shots. However, as soon as they climb down into a bunker, they find a new arena and the rules change. Now they can use their collapsing left wrist effectively.

Bunker play is a different game. But the differences are in your favor if your leading wrist usually collapses at impact. In the bunker, instructors *want* you to collapse the wrist so that you can bring the open face of your wedge sliding under the ball with the left-hand palm down in the collapsed position.

This wrist position works for flop shots out of the deep rough too, but you'll need a flat and arched left wrist for everything else.

At address, your weight is on the left foot. The stance is open. The leading palm can be turned to the ground by collapsing the left wrist even before swinging into the impact spot two inches behind the ball. This is why so many amateur golfers are not that bad in a trap—the left hand collapses, or is held in the collapsed position (left palm down) and the open club face slides under the ball.

Note the almost straight line from right shoulder to right hand and club face—completely opposite to a shot from the grass.

The bunker shot can best be described as an arm-and-hand shot. Nothing else moves much. Certainly not your flexed legs. You're just sitting there on the bar stool. Your hands are hovering *behind* the ball. Your body is aligned to an "open" toe line to approximate the impact position. Your shoulders tilt back down the target line for the steep take-away, then down the target line for the "splash" down behind the ball.

The golfer's toes, knees, and hips are "open" to the target line simulating the impact position. It has to be simulated because the lower body does not go through the usual rotation during a sand shot. This can be called a "hands and arm" shot. The shoulders follow the target line, tilting down, then up, with the club face wide open.

The feet should be wide apart for stability. Dig in (even shorten the grip) to get your feet on the same level as the ball. Your feet are in the open position to anticipate the hip position at impact. Make these adjustments now, so that you don't have to move anything below the waist during the shot—although the right knee can follow the hands through the ball.

Weight on the lead splayed foot is to approximate the impact position and you are ready for the first move. Your feet and knees match the angle of the toe line which is about thirty degrees "open" from the target line. Your hands and arms follow the target line.

Notice that you have been comfortable with the club not touching the sand—this confidence might encourage you to "hover" the club head in similar fashion for putting and driving, and certainly out of the rough.

The first move of the take-away is to cock the wrists with a steep upward angle. There is no extension back down the target line as with a shot from the fairway. Stay still from the waist down.

The golfer's weight is on the lead foot, and where the weight is tells you where the bottom of the club-face arc is. Your body points to the ball (your chest center and belt buckle do not move laterally).

The take-away for the bunker shot is an immediate cocking of the right wrist back along the target line. Leave your right elbow hugging the rib cage for strong connection to ensure the accurate return of the club face to its position at address.

In the high point of backswing, thinking only of where the ball should land.

Accelerate through the ball. To increase the loft, strengthen the grip by turning the left hand clockwise.

For a running ball, weaken the grip by turning the left hand counter clockwise. Use a nine iron for longer shots. Also, remember that the higher the follow-through, the further the ball will run (the hardest bunker shot is the long one, and few golfers get the ball to the pin).

Now with your Viking-axe smash, whack the open face two inches behind the ball and let the "palm down" leading wrist pass right under the ball. With this action the open club face will thump down on the chosen spot, and will splash the ball high and happy to the pin.

The follow-through has two discussion points. The first asks whether you use the usual Hogan finish with the right palm facing the target, or his finish for softer shots with the right palm facing the sky.

The higher the finish, the further the ball will travel. After a "shortish" backswing, a high follow-through will ensure that there is no deceleration (of course you've already learned that from the putting section).

Right hand splash down.

High finish for distance.

Drill

Climb into a deep bunker far away from the club house windows, and try this "stationary body" but active right-arm shot with the left arm out of the picture.

Feel the right elbow on the pelvic crest. Aim the center of your right hand to the spot in the sand where you're aiming.

One-armed shots will give you a better feel for the application, and perhaps confidence, needed when you find that this is indeed a one-armed shot.

When you get the right-hand-only shot working fairly well, call on your left hand—palm down—*behind* the ball and leave it collapsed, with the left palm facing the ground as your right hand splashes down and under the ball.

One-hand connected take-away.

In a bunker, the shoulder position and stance are open in order to imitate the impact posture without using lower body movement and to accommodate the necessity for remaining still.

A one-hand connected splash through. A few of these should give you some confidence, or a signal to book a lesson from your pro.

According to at least two caddies, Ben Hogan did not get into many bunkers—his course management was too advanced—but when he erred, he could handle himself all right.

Gary Player on the other hand was hailed as a great bunker player and was said to finish the day's drill on the practice area in a bunker splashing out balls until he sunk one. Sandy Lyle of Scotland scoffed at the thought of sinking only one, and Moe Norman hit until he filled his two or three targeted cups.

Gary Player had a laugh with David Feherty during an interview when he remembered one day as a rookie when Ben Hogan stopped by to watch Player practicing in the trap.

"Hello," Hogan said to me—"you'll be good one day. Do you practice hard?"

"I touched my cap and answered: 'Yes Mr. Hogan'.... I wanted to say 'as hard as you'...but I didn't."

PHOTO COURTESY OF AP IMAGES

Note that for this particular shot Hogan kept his left palm pointing to the sand in order to keep the club face wide open for a softer shot.

WHEN SWEET SPOTS COLLIDE

A "sweet spot" refers to the center of gravity within any material body that can be seen or touched—even an object as small as a golf ball—and that center of gravity is weightless and without mass. It is simply the center, but when that sweet spot within the head of your golf club collides with the sweet spot in the center of your golf ball, memorable things can happen.

A straight line to the center of gravity from the surface of the club to the ball is called the "center of percussion," and as I understand, the physics applied to the golf hit—with physics not my subject at all—this is the point which absorbs the most energy. That observation means that the squarely struck ball is given greater velocity because the force goes in a straight line through the center of percussion to the center of gravity.

All I know is the memory of the first time I experienced this very satisfying event—the sound, the feel, the launch. I was eleven, and had a three-hole pitch and putt course in my grandfather's double lot without a lane. However, even with this extra large backyard, I had the urge to whack a long shot, and convinced myself that if I hit my Tom Auchterlonie hand-made, hickory-shafted mashie niblick...well, the ball would sail over the vacant lot beside our yard, to land harmlessly in the intersection where Thirty-Fourth Avenue crossed Blenheim Street, and that I would get a thrill. I was sort of right.

So I waited until sure there were no cars, and swung freely. At once there was "a special feeling running from my hands, up my arms and into my heart," as Mr. Hogan would say one day. It was breathtaking as I watched the ball soar straight and true, but for some reason it was still rising as it cleared the intersection. I was aghast. My best shot ever...and there it was, high over the intersection heading directly toward the middle of the living room window at Mrs. Laural's house on the corner!

I dropped down below the rock wall—hand-built by my grandfather—and listened, waiting for the expensive sound of crashing glass.

Nothing. There was nothing! No shattering glass. No angry voices. I raised my head cautiously. Still nothing. Then finally got up enough nerve to sneak up to the house looking for my near-new U.S. Royal golf ball. Where was it? Not on the lawn. Nowhere to be seen, until I followed the line of flight and looked in the center of the eight-foot-long flower box which ran the length of the window. There was my ball plugged in the dirt amid the geraniums.

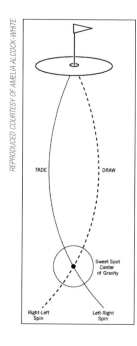

The best tip I learned from Ted Kroll was the need to deliver the sweet spot on the face of my club, through "one dimple" at the back of the golf ball in a direct line to the center of gravity. He claimed that Hogan used two main "tricks" to increase the probability for repeating that lovely moment of sound and "feel" when the sweet spots collide— a perfect and powerful contact.

These two "tricks" are done within the golfer's imagination and are best learned while putting. First, he thinks of a black spot on the back of his left hand. Second, when the left shoulder pushes the hands into a take-away, he is aware that the black dot is pointing back down at the imagined dimple on the back of the ball.

A variation on this, while hitting half-shots for example, is to pretend that the head of your nine iron is taped onto the palm of your right hand, with a dot on the sweet spot— and that is what you are returning to that "specific dimple" on the back of the ball.

For the longer shafts, the sweet spot is in the center of the right palm, and you are going to drive that spot into the "center of percussion" on the back of the ball. You can watch yourself do this in front of a mirror.

Or better yet, while you're waiting for dinner, chip down the rug in the hall while concentrating on the spot in the middle of your right hand. The cook won't mind, because she's probably admiring your dedication to golf as an art form.

Here are some other thoughts you should explore to see which ones suit you.

The center of percussion aims a straight, narrow line into the ball's center of gravity. The golfer's shoulder line influences the path of the ball by pulling the slightly lofted putter along the chosen alignment of the shoulders, and thereby facilitating a straight, hook, or slice putt. This next diagram is worth your study.

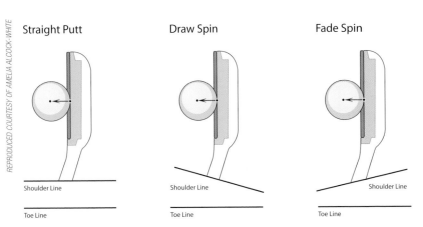

Straight Putt   Draw Spin   Fade Spin

Shoulder Line   Shoulder Line   Shoulder Line

Toe Line   Toe Line   Toe Line

Every line is square to the target line, except the "open" shoulder line and the "closed" shoulder line. Put a tee peg in the green and get "involved" with the concepts within this diagram. The "straight-on" putt image is very effective. The others are for special moments—like "holding" the line against the break. You will expand your imagination markedly by using this guide.

With this diagram in mind, try staring down at the top of the ball and pick out the dimple directly above the center of gravity. Then, imagine the arrow in the diagram extending from the sweet spot on the top of your putter blade. In your mind's eye this sharp arrow is going to spear through the back of the ball directly toward and into the ball's center of gravity. It could be a useful image for you.

The "hook" putt, used by many of the great putters like Bobby Locke, is influenced by the pull of the lead shoulder, this time from a closed position at address. Many players execute the right to left spin on the "hooking" ball with their hands, and you can hear them mention to one another the need for "letting the toe pass over" the far edge of the ball. However, one must remember that it is very difficult to control the hands when nerves are "jangling." The big muscles of the shoulders can offer a far greater degree of reliability for repeating the stroke. Changing the shoulder line to closed, open, or square determines direction of spin. Try it during the drill putting to a tee.

For short putts which are relatively flat, the straight shot is preferred. For this putt the center of percussion line to the target is paralleled by the "square" alignment of shoulders, hips, and knees. Now the direction lines from both sweet spots are traveling in the same direction. With a squarely struck putt—where the follow-through does not decelerate—both sweet spots collide with only one way for the energy to go: straight.

Now here's another thought for you to consider at length: from a square stance, hit it straight, with topspin. Hogan claimed that the bottom of a club head's arc occurs where most of the weight has settled. That observation means that once you've established where the bottom of the arc is, position the ball a bit forward. If you have the putter hovered, you will bring the sweet spot on your club's face in a "rising" path to the ball's center of percussion. Voila! You get a straight putt with overspin.

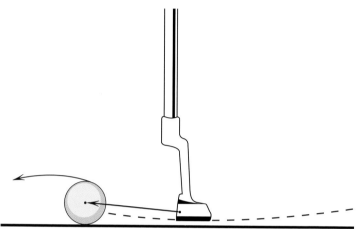

The club's face is above the grass, and from the lowest point of the club's arc, is moving toward the ball's "center of percussion" in a "low to higher angle." This is a good diagram to dwell upon while drill-putting to a tee on the practice green—not a cup, please. Use the cup for competitions—using only one ball—everything holed.

TIP 7

PLAYING IN PRO-AMS

There's plenty of equipment to try.

If you ever want a great time on the golf course, surrounded by drama within unfolding stories of triumph and disaster, pony up a little cash—which will be given back to you in gifts and tax receipts—and enjoy a great time for amateur golfers from good-to-medium skill levels. For any golfer this really is a great, great, great experience. You'll meet some wonderful like-minded people.

Take Bing Crosby as one example. When World War Two finally ended in 1945, I was twelve. My father had been in Europe with the Canadian Army for more than five years and was not home yet...and along came Bing Crosby with those gentle, fatherly eyes. He was on a salmon fishing trip to Campbell River, but came to Point Grey first for a little golf, and I was drawn to caddie for him. What a thrill. He looked like my father and acted like my father. For me the round was over far too quickly. Then, with clubs in the car he handed me a shiny blue five dollar bill and thanked me for my work. I was stunned. The looper's fee was one dollar not five. Besides, I didn't want to charge him. I was very content in his company.

I handed back the five dollar bill trying to explain. "No Mr. Crosby...please, it's my treat...it was...nice."

The famous blue eyes studied me for a moment. He seemed to know all about me, and said: "OK. But let's do it this way. You hang on to this bill, just don't do anything with it. Keep it tucked away for something special. And when the right moment comes along you'll have it ready."

As if in a dream, this made sense somehow, and I nodded as I shook his hand. Then watched him drive away.

PHOTO COURTESY OF AP IMAGES

Tree trouble for Bing on the 18th hole at Cypress Point. But he and partner Ben Hogan still managed a "tidy" 63 net.

It was not until years later that I got to spend that five dollars. Sent down to the Crosby National Pro-Am by the *Vancouver Sun* as a freelance writer, I met Bing's widow, Kathryn Crosby, and she thanked me for some photographs I'd sent from the previous year's "Clambake." She heard that I had caddied for Bing, and the next thing I knew I had an invitation to the "greatest golf show on earth."

A close friend living nearby the Monterey Peninsula was a volunteer marshal, with the good sense to book practice tee times for me at the three courses on the rotation list. I had booked off for the next week (without pay of course) and would leave school in Vancouver soon after Friday's 3:15 bell, and head for the airport very keen to arrive in Monterey that evening, ready to play the practice schedule "good old Pete" had arranged before the first competitive rounds began the next Thursday. The scores for Thursday, Friday, and Saturday on the three famous courses would determine the final cut for the pro-am teams which were to be played at Pebble Beach on Sunday. Some famous people tried like hell to play on Sunday with their pro, so practice was important. This is the schedule Pete had arranged for me:

	8 a.m.	2 p.m.
Saturday:	Cypress Point	Pebble Beach
Sunday:	Spyglass Hill	Cypress Point
Monday:	Cypress Point	Pebble Beach
Tuesday:	Spyglass Hill	Cypress Point
Wednesday:	Cypress Point	Pebble Beach

Talk about falling into a good thing; it was indeed "Golf Heaven." Not only did Pete book a great "practice" timetable, but I also found that there were unexpected perks on the horizon. It seemed that very few amateur guests had caddies astute enough to book tee times, and so, invariably, for the three years which followed—because I was playing alone—the starter would, without fail, come over. "Excuse me," he would begin amiably, "would you mind if those three gentlemen joined you?" He would glance over to three professionals who would be standing at a distance looking me up and down and, I would reply as graciously as I could, "Certainly, please invite them along."

Thus over three wonderful years I got to tee it up with some great players: Tom Kite, Davis Love III, Corey Pavin, Jim Thorpe, Paul Azinger, Dick Zokol, Jim Furyk, Brad Faxon, Joey Sindelar, and Hal Sutton. I watched for the right moment before asking anyone about Hogan, but they all had opinions and stories. As my grandfather had once predicted: "There will be days when you'd like to live forever."

And so it was that first year, failing to "make the cut," I found myself in the Lodge's Cypress Grill for brunch on the Sunday. Giant pastel paintings of the Californian coastline and Big Sur dominated the spacious room overlooking the eighteenth green and Still Water Cove. In the amphitheatre dining room, four chefs stood at the top level ready to prepare any culinary request, while a Russian piano player in black suit and tie played a resonant grand piano. This was certainly the civilized way to dine. On my way to the chef, I walked past the pianist and asked if he might play Schubert's *Serenade* that morning. He smiled with a bow, as he continued with *Rhapsody in Blue*.

Later, when he saw that I had my tea, he caught my eye and nodded before beginning my request. I reveled in the atmosphere, and wondered how I might mark this special time in order to hold it in my memory bank for the next 100 years. I remembered my time with the fatherly Bing Crosby...and I knew.

As I left that special place, I approached the pianist. "Maestro," I said quietly, "You were at your best. Thank you. You've filled my day."

With a smile he offered his hand. I took it, palming him Crosby's five dollar bill. That moment felt very good.

Pro-am golf tournaments were started during the bleak days of the "Dirty Thirties" when young players like Ben Hogan, Sam Snead, and Byron Nelson traveled the "Gold Trail," often waiting a long time for the gold to appear. Then celebrities like Bing Crosby, Bob Hope, and Dinah Shore got into the act, and their presence attracted commercial sponsors who recognized the potential for publicity wrapped in a lot of fun.

Now pro-ams are part of every recognized golf event all over the world from Dubai to Singapore, to Melbourne and Christchurch. The biggest winners are without a doubt the thousands of charities benefitting from a challenging and happy event. The golfers pick up an attractive source of extra income—even if they can't make the cut for the real money. Win a tournament now, and you're a millionaire—Sam Snead, with the most professional wins when the top prize was $2,000—is likely rolling over in his grave noting the top prizes in the twenty-first century. And Ben Hogan is shaking his head, remembering stealing oranges from the California orchards for food and winning $75 in his first Crosby Pro-Am.

Some Things to Keep in Mind When Playing in a Pro-Am

1. Don't fuss about your shot—nobody really cares what your swing looks like. Nobody expects a fantastic stroke. There are 154.7 million people in Bangladesh who couldn't care less...and your pro partner is only a couple of paces out of that category of caring.

2. Be ready to play when your turn comes up—don't stand watching someone else. Have the yardage figured out, and be ready to go. Give it no more than one practice swing, look hard at the target then hit the ball.

3. When you've played your shot, walk quickly down the fairway; find your ball and hit it again—repeating the routine described above in number 2. You'll probably be surprised at how fast the pros walk to their next shot.

4. Play as if you care only that your companions do well.

5. While approaching greens, take a quick view for the "fall-line" a ball would take if rolling to the hole. Your first impression of the line is mostly your best. Don't ask the caddie for his "vision"—it's your image that you putt to. Besides, "weight" is more important than line. And please don't pull a Tiger and stalk around a 360-degree circle tying to decide God knows what. What was it that Gene Sarazen would say? "Miss 'em quick."

6. Still on the green, where do you stand when another is putting? The answer sounds complicated but it's simple...and fool proof, if you think about it for a minute.

Good golfers, like the two pros you'll be playing with, are trying to "visualize" the ball's tracking to the target and so, whether on or off the green, stay out of their sight. If you can see their eyes, they can see you—and that's like changing channels in the middle of their swing.

So where do you stand? Try this—stand anywhere on the "latitude" they are standing on. Latitude would be perpendicular to the putter's target line. That is, directly behind, or directly in front of the player about to hit.

If you can determine who putts next, and from where, you can be in place before they are ready to putt. You'll be looking at their backside from behind them, or the top of their head if in front. Either place, you can't see their eyes and they can't see you. As a result, they will not be worrying about you making some movement during their swing, and will relax in your company. All of sudden you'll find that they are really good guys who have accepted you, and you realize that you're having a good time. A few of my club colleagues complain about the cold personality their pro had. Chances are they were standing in his range of vision.

Not every pro will tell you if something you are doing bothers them, so it's best to know the possibilities beforehand. When I first played with Jim Thorpe—born in North Carolina and a former running back for Morgan State University—he sure enough looked like a tough ex–football player.

Jim had it teed up on the second hole at Spyglass, while I stood quietly further back in the tee looking right down his line of sight to the green. All of a sudden I was aware that he was gliding silently up to me like a stalking leopard. His eyes were fixed with the stare of a hypnotist. The shape of his nose spoke of the hard old days as he pushed his face close to my mine. "Are you sure you want to stand there?" he asked in a growl.

"No...no, pro. Where do you want me to stand?" I asked, trying not to stammer.

It was then I first heard the suggestion/request/command: "Stand on my latitude."

And Thorpe was right. If I stood in front of him on an extended line from the shaft of his club, I was staring at the top of his head. He couldn't see me.

And it was the same if I stood behind him looking at his backside...he couldn't see me. Where it was distracting for him was when the onlooker could see his left eye. From there you are interfering with the "vision" of his target, he's thinking of you and not the flight of the ball he is about to send along a chosen path.

PHOTO COURTESY OF MIKE LILLY

Amid the clutter of the practice range, Stewart Cink hovers his driver for a smooth take-away.

If playing in the pro-am is a bit daunting for you, there are still dozens of good jobs that will fill your days at the tournament with excitement and atmosphere:

- Work on the scoreboard if you're good with numbers.
- Keep players supplied with practice balls at the driving range. You'll meet all the players. You'll get to see their swings up close. And some of those new Titleist balls might find their way into your bag before the week is over.
- Driving players to and fro in the donated cars is a chance to talk to them in a private setting where private ques-

tions are more likely to be answered. Gossip is always interesting as you drive to and from the course.

• If you don't mind walking within the ropes, volunteer as a marshal or a scoreboard carrier. You'll see and hear lots of things people back home won't see on TV.

PHOTO COURTESY OF MEL ZAJAC

Bob Hope, a noted golf addict during his Palm Desert Classic days, celebrates a good shot. On the golf course away from the crowd he was amazingly restrained, and quietly full of questions.

Davis Love III showing the gallery his warm-up routine before the Monterey Boys and Girls Club Charity Pro-Am.

Michelle Wie at the Canadian Women's Championship, in the Media Tent at Vancouver Golf Club.

PHOTO COURTESY OF BURRARD INTERNATIONAL

Jack Nicklaus opening "Nicklaus North," one of his designs near the beautiful Whistler Ski Resort site of the 2010 Winter Olympics.

Pro-ams are really a good experience for a volunteer worker. They give you a uniform you can keep to bring out for "show" on special occasions at your club. There's plenty of food and drink. And you are "inside the ropes" where the action is, crowded with conversations and the vibrations of adventure. But best of all, on a growing number of fine courses, Monday is closed to members for volunteers to play a round.

Here's a clever addition to the LPGA golf tour. Michelle Wie sits outside the media tent entertaining informal questions from fans.

DOWN FROM THE
TOP—BELOW THE WAIST

PHOTO COURTESY OF MIKE LILLY

Look at the result of Davis Love's coil. Not a big man, DL3—as the caddies call him—has been a long-ball hitter for most of his career. That left heel (like Nicklaus) is about to drop, and the left knee will then lead the upper body into action.

Ask almost any amateur golfer the question, "What is your first move down from the top of your backswing?" Invariably you'll get a blank expression followed by a question: "My hands?"

Wrong! The first move down is a tricky little sequence, but valuable in the extreme. Remember in Tip 3 the first move down from a half backswing for a pitch or lob was "simplified" into both the left shoulder and the left hip moving the triangle toward impact at the same time?

Well, for the long shots it's a bit more complicated. From the top of the backswing there should be a separation of the golfer's body into two parts—the bottom half, and the top. For an accomplished golfer, both parts have different actions that blend in the flash of a second—but the bottom half leads the way.

The bottom half moves more like a counter-clockwise merry-go-round. The top half moves somewhat like a "teeter-totter" or tilting board; if they don't separate, the golfer joins the ranks of the frustrated and mystified as to where the ball might fly. Separation is worth learning.

It sounds a bit crazy, but the first move down occurs before the hands get to the very top (but who ever said that golf makes a lot of sense?). The golf swing is full of contradictions, but understanding them gives one blips of occasional satisfaction. So, as Q would say to James Bond, "Pay attention 007. This is important." You should learn this "progressive flow of action" because you might find out how you too can hit the ball toward the target more often.

Try this next sequence, in slow motion in front of a mirror, and you'll know the answer for keeps: at the top of the golf swing for a full shot, the left knee has pushed in toward the stationary right knee, and has thereby "loaded" some extra weight onto the inside edge of the golfer's right foot.

The tempo for the turn to this top position has been smooth and "controlled"—think Ernie Els—but don't worry, things will speed up momentarily. For now you want a smooth, slowish tempo for two reasons:

1. You don't have to hit anything on the backswing, but more importantly,
2. You should always "complete the backswing."

When you finish the backswing properly, the golfer doesn't give away any of the wound-up power which produces distance.

PHOTO COURTESY OF D. DWYER

Here Hogan has just about reached the top. The left knee is turning in toward the center of the stance and the right elbow is losing its connection to the rib cage.

Because the right knee is flexed and stationary (and there is no "swaying" or "sliding" to release muscle tension) the golfer feels the "wound up" tension of the muscles across the back and shoulders—when at the top, you should not be able to breathe or speak.

The left shoulder turns to a point just behind the ball, and the hands have just about reached the top of the swing. And while this stretch upward continues, the large back muscles are wound up toward their limit, and this is a signal that the left side is about to receive the preponderance of weight, pressed into the inside edge of the right shoe by a rotating action of the knees.

It is at this point that the first move down from the top begins, and it is the job of the lower half of the body to lead the way—not the hands.

The left knee, turned in toward the center of the stance, returns to the address position with the left foot back over the flat left shoe so that the knees are separated. All in a fraction of a second, the golfer is in the "bar-stool" position just as the hands reach up to the maximum point of their "full shot" stretch.

Now the flexed left knee begins a "grinding" turn, pulled by the left hip and the large muscles of the thighs and buttocks, and the flexed right knee follows. This "deliberate" move is, in turn, a signal to the left shoulder to rise up one more notch even though you thought that the shoulder was at its peak—and magically, the right elbow returns to its connected position on the crest of the pelvis.

Notice that the left shoulder is raised up from under the golfer's chin, to alongside the chin. The knees are now in tandem and grinding past the ball toward the target. The left hip is pulling out of the way. The bottom has separated from the top with the challenge: "Chase me!"

From these two photos you will notice that the three-point "connection" at mid-swing is broken at the top. The right elbow has become disconnected. Golfers are usually intent on a "speedy" lash at the ball...but they must learn that for a solid hit from a well-directed club face nailing the ball on the sweet spot. "Job one" is to get that connection back in place. And the re-connection is so easy, you'll wonder why you've ignored it for so long while wondering why you come over the top so regularly.

Here's the quick fix in front of a mirror. Take your imaginary club to the top of the backswing and watch your right elbow pull away from the rib cage. Now, as your flexed knees begin grinding toward the target, just raise your left shoulder—I know you think it's high now—but just push straight up one more notch from under your chin to ear level, and look what has happened so easily: your right elbow is now connected to the right side of your torso. Also, you are sitting on the bar stool.

At the first moment of the left shoulder rise, there is an instantaneous change of speed from "medium" to "fast forward," as the hips—as quickly as possible, for a long shot—turn the golfers belt buckle to the target, counter clockwise. There is no "sliding" toward the target, only a "turning in a barrel," without touching the sides of the barrel. The right forearm is attached to the right hip which drives the forearm as a "fulcrum" toward impact with the ball.

Now, with the triangle fully connected again over a balanced "athletic stance," the engaged abdominal muscles turn the hips—with great power and speed—through the contact zone. That's a lot of detail happening in the space of a second and a bit. But this is the sequence and timing for those beautiful swings you see on television.

Let's get this complex series into a tidy list, and from there, clear enough in your mind that you can close your eyes at the dentist or barber, and "see" the moves.

1. On the take-away, the left knee moves inward toward the stationary right knee.
2. Full tension on the right flank signals the left knee to return to its flexed position over the flat left foot. The left knee can return to its address position with a separate move, or it can move in tandem with the right knee, pulled by the left hip and thigh, while the right knee is "pushed" by the right thigh.

3. When the left hip begins to rotate counter clockwise, the knees separate the action of the lower body from the action of the upper body.

4. As the left knee returns to the inside edge of the golfer's left foot, it is a signal to the left shoulder to rise one more notch, straight up. With this last tilt, you will find that the connection has returned to the right elbow on the right pelvic crest.

5. Now the controlled tempo is no longer useful—this is "rip it" time—and the belt buckle turns with speed, with the abdominal muscles fully engaged.

6. All this happens within the space of grass between the golfer's "toe line" and the "target line" that we can refer to as the "infield." The strongest point here is that neither the hands nor the right shoulder have gone "over the top" of the ball toward the "outfield"—no doubt the primary cause of some wicked shots.

PHOTO COURTESY OF LINDA LEONARD

On the first tilt down by Stan Leonard, we get a clear sense that this re-attachment is the silent signal for the real action to begin as the right side—shoulder, hip, and knee "drive hard" under the ball, pulled by the muscles of the torso. There is a sense of the power unleashed, as his right hip helps the "core" drive a molded hand-set into the ball.

Drill Focus

Practice half-wedge shots while concentrating on holding the right elbow on the crest of the right pelvis as you rotate your hips through the ball. The center of the chest stays behind the ball.

As you get the hang of it, speed up the torso through the strike and concentrate on getting the "right side" under the ball. Then extend the club's shaft pointing down the target line.

When your belt buckle turns into the ball, the force of the strike will "drag" your fulcrum arm "across" your abdomen toward the belly button...so the upper arm moves, but it does not lose its connection with the torso as it slides across your chest.

A bad shot to the right might happen to you, but you'll know how to correct it—keep your right elbow connected to your turning torso.

PHOTO COURTESY OF JULES ALEXANDER

This photo has the look of power in balance. There is also the promise of speed with the turning left hip followed by the thrusting right hip and the "hit" with right shoulder. Just look at the "right side" connection. Glue your elbow to the right side and turn your hips through the ball—knuckles down.

Jules Alexander, the man who took this photograph, remembers that when Mr. Hogan hit a good shot to a faraway green he could be heard saying to his caddie, "Heaven is a long walk with the putter."

Mirror Drill

Here's a quick way to develop good "foot" action to go with your stable right knee. Sam Snead used to preach that we should all play some casual golf in bare feet so that we could better learn the "grinding" circular action of the lower body during a shot.

The best lesson to learn from this exercise is that the first move down from the top of any golf shot is the left knee returning to its address position. This action separates the lower body from the upper body, as the knees begin their counter-clockwise motion into the impact zone.

Watch Tiger on TV settle into the "bar stool" position as his knees start grinding around a power platform. His hands can't catch up.

Don't tell casual friends you're doing this, but just before bed, get in front of a full-length mirror and address an imaginary ball as if for a three-quarter golf shot, while you "position" the right knee—pushed in just a bit toward the centre of your stance.

Now turn the hips slowly away from the ball in the first stage of the take-away, and watch as the left knee begins to reach toward the center of the stance. The right knee does not move from its flexed address position—weight on the inside edge of your foot.

Both knees are flexed in an "athletic" position. The hands are at the proper grip angles. They are separated to show you that they aren't moving by themselves. You could cheat if you want, but the drill won't be doing you much good. Your shoulder connection moves the hands.

The hands are being pushed by the triangle and do not move on their own.

However, the flexed left knee does move quietly in toward the center of the stance as the hands extend back down the target line away from the ball.

When your hands reach the stationary right knee, the wrists hinge as they continue to rise to three-quarter position.

Palms face each other at the hinging point.
The left knee has pressed in.

When it's time to bring the hands down toward the ball, the hips begin to rotate out of the way of the molded hands and the left knee moves back to the address position. Raise your left shoulder to "tilt" the shoulder and arm triangle, so that your right elbow drops onto your hip.

The rising of the left shoulder is a signal to the right knee to drive under the ball toward the target, and to push the left knee toward the target as the hips turn hard and fast—counter clockwise—with the knees remaining flexed. The left hip turns counter clockwise away from the target and not sliding toward it.

The right knee is ready to move under the ball.

Hands have not moved on their own. The right hand arches down to the ball but does not pronate.

Now the "rotation to impact" speeds up with the engaged abdominal core and the right side turning through the ball with the fastest move of the entire swing.

The belt buckle turns to face the target. The knees still have some flex, and the left foot is flat on the floor. Good balance is the result.

TIP 9

DOWN FROM THE TOP—ABOVE THE WAIST

Hogan was adamant about maintaining a strong and well-balanced foundation because of the vigorous swing demanded for the driver—as well as most other long-shafted clubs when performing full shots. Balance was key. Amateurs did not, in his opinion, pay enough attention to their alignment by a simple action which, in order to check or correct their position for balance, demanded nothing more than watching one's shadow with the sun at your back before the shot is taken. Get the sun behind you for a practice stretch and show yourself a stability that keeps the spine of your shadow rotating in place, and not wavering to the right or left—a properly positioned right knee being the biggest stabilizing influence.

The "secure feel" the golfer should "fan into flame" can be reviewed quietly while others tee off. Get off by yourself—behind them on their latitude—and revisit the centered alignment you want when the face of the driver impacts the ball.

"Stay behind the ball" is the usual instruction, or "rotate around your spine" is another useful piece of advice. Perhaps a few more details might increase the likelihood of your success, such as: "Keep your belt buckle and the 'third button on your shirt' in line with the ball at address."

Camilo Villegas has all the diamonds on his sweater lined up to stay behind the ball through the impact phase.

Some golfers prefer to be very specific and more personal. They can visualize better that way. Two good reference points are: high on your chest in the center of your "breast plate" (sternum), and your "belly button" (umbilicus)—both are set up even with the ball, and then kept in that relationship throughout impact.

Perhaps even more "graphic" for some, is the alignment of "symphysis pubis." (Google will clarify: "The pubic symphysis is a cartilaginous joint that forms the median junction of the two pubic bones.") With that little bar of cartilage pointing to the back of the ball, the golfer has a subtle and personal sense of the lower point that should remain pointing at the ball, along with the heart—its "higher up" partner between the breasts—when making certain to "stay behind the ball."

This alignment will keep the golfer from swaying the center of the swing away from the ball. Also, this alignment will greatly improve accuracy, and so it would be prudent to check your line-up as part of a regular routine. Add a flexed but stationary right knee to "secure" this alignment...and you're ready.

The final detail placed upon this solid foundational structure is the "fulcrum" created by the golfer's right forearm and its "connection" with the area near the right pelvic crest. For shorter half-shots it's quite easy to maintain connection because of the abbreviated take-away. But for the longer shots there will be a "disconnection" at top of the backswing which is, as you now know, easily replaced by an upward tilt of the dominating left shoulder.

A great many golfers understand that if they "decelerate" during the forward stroke in putting, the ball won't make it to the hole. This is true because, if you decelerate at all, you will most certainly begin the slowing process long before the club face arrives at impact. When this early slowing occurs, you will lose a significant amount of roll. Hopefully, you will have learned this truism from your putting sessions, and have made suitable adjustments for it by extending after the ball when it has left for the target.

If you have learned not to decelerate when putting, then you will know that the follow-through in putting must continue long after the "hit" in order to get the full velocity into the ball—a velocity which has been "calculated" and planned by your brain while sizing up the distance to the hole. If you aren't getting the ball at least one foot past the cup putting, you are likely decelerating.

The same thing occurs with a full shot. Your unabated follow-through must go well past the impact point. If you do follow through correctly, it means that your right side has gone "fully" past the ball's position on the tee, and that the body has reacted to this fact. As a result, you will recognize that your belt buckle is square to the hole; your hip line is square to the target; and that you have released the power of the right knee into the shot so completely, that you are balanced in a high follow-through with weight almost fully upon the flat left foot. Your right side is balanced on the back foot's "dirty toe."

PHOTO COURTESY OF PETER KAZAKOFF

At twelve years of age, Callie—whose proud grandfather was my caddie for three Crosby Pro-Ams—finds no problem with this graceful move showing her athletic balance.

Stan Leonard learned from Hogan that a "prelude practice swing" was an effective rehearsal which would ensure a full follow-through to the top.

He would hold the club head above and inside the teed ball, before slowly swinging the club head forward, half-way toward the hole, then swing the club slowly past the teed ball, half-way back down the target line as for a take-away. When there, he would turn his upper body to a high follow-through position—with a slight pause for a laser-like stare at the target. After "taking the picture" he would return the club head to its elevated address position, and begin the actual swing for the shot.

False address position. Club well away from the ball.

Swinging forward past the left knee.

Swinging back to right knee.

Swinging high to finish.

Leonard would hold the "warm-up" pose in a high finish for an instant, then get back to the address position with the muscle memory of his finish position still "glowing."

When he was ready to launch, he would, without wasting any time, address the ball, review the personal photo of his chosen line to the target, then begin his real backswing for the shot. In his mind he remembered the target. In his muscles he could "feel" the practice swing's highest point. Then he would swing through impact and up to the rehearsed full follow-through position.

PHOTO COURTESY OF MIKE LILLY

Here is Fred Couples in one of his languid, high finishes in relaxed athletic balance.

TIP 10

PLAYING WITH STRENGTH FROM A SOLID BASE

PHOTO COURTESY OF ALVIE THOMPSON

Moe Norman's knees have begun the downswing. When that left shoulder rises, the elbow will be connected again and the turn through the ball will begin with great speed and power from that textbook foundation.

Following the "move from the top," the golfer should, at the very least, come close to the power structure we see with Moe Norman at Richmond Golf Club during the Vancouver Open in 1960. With this foundation for hitting the ball, Moe looks as much like a defensive line-backer as a golfer about to "powder" the ball.

A wide stance provides unshakable balance. As you can see, he is starting to complete the task of returning his right elbow to a connected position on the right side. He has just settled into a position commonly referred to as "sitting on the bar stool." There is a wide separation of the two flexed knees—a separation touted by the great Sam Snead.

Moe's swing was so rapid—from address to through-swing—that watchers were not aware of the forceful "knee action" that we can see on "super slow-motion" films now, and many had supposed he kept his legs straight throughout the entire procedure, as he showed at address.

The left knee, still flexed, has moved back to its "address" position. The returned weight is on the flat left foot—from the big toe to the heel—from its position at the top of the backswing while the golfer's right side "loaded up" onto the inside edge of the right shoe.

Notice that Moe's head has not moved significantly during the "sit down" move, as the golfer prepares a solid foundation for the striking of the ball.

Tiger "sits on the bar stool" for every shot. There was a period in 2012 when his head moved to the right, and down, as the left shoulder went up, and some wild shots interrupted the majesty of his body shift into the two separated parts. In the brilliant opening of the 2013 season he held his head steady under the tilting triangle of shoulders and arms trying to catch the leading lower hips circling and driving the fulcrum into the ball. Result? Five wins.

With the shoulder triangle moving separately, the balanced foundation, as demonstrated by Hogan below, is more easily attained.

Hogan is now ready to turn his belt buckle through the impact zone driven by his knees and counter-rotating hips. The strength of the torso turns the connected shoulder structure into the ball with speed.

The power released from this "bar stool" position becomes more apparent when you imagine what body movement would be required to throw a medicine ball across the room. The arm swingers would not get as much force and distance as the "chuckers" who engage the big muscles in the thighs, bum, and tummy. Take another look at "Bantam" Ben Hogan and think about what he did with his 145 pounds on a five-foot, eight-inch frame. He used his torso strength, and became recognized as one of the long drivers on tour. In fact, at Carnoustie Hogan won the 1953 Open Championships by accomplishing four two-putt birdies over the seventy-two-hole ordeal. His birdies came on the sixth hole, a 512-yard par five with an out of bounds fence down the left side, just five yards from a nasty line of pot bunkers. Most pros hit a four iron from the tee, followed by a seven, then a nine, guaranteed to reach the green in three shots for a "safe par." Hogan took driver down the five-yard-wide stretch of grass along the OB fence, then hit three wood to the green, followed by a putt-putt for birdie. He won the Claret Jug by two shots and they put a plaque on the sixth tee, re-naming the "Long Hole," "Hogan's Alley."

Every year the club puts on a "Long Drive Contest" using equipment from Hogan's era including the elastic-wound ball. Players are astounded to find themselves fifty yards short of Bantam Ben's 280-yard drives. One year the long-drive was won by Vijay Singh at 238 yards while Colin Montgomerie plastered his elastic-wound Titleist 218 yards.

How did Hogan do this? Well, for the distance part, he used the strength of his torso. And how do you do this? Lee Trevino suggests that anyone who wants to get stronger and better, should hit 300 balls per day. We know that for most folks this is impossible. However, a regime of 300 "abdominal crunches" per day is doable—legs bent; feet flat on the floor; arms crossed over chest; then, watching television ads between your knees, raise your shoulders four inches off the floor with a contraction of your core. Start with ten repetitions in three sets, then build up to 100 reps in three sets to total 300 crunches. These will make a big differences in your ability to play this curious game.

"Plank" exercises will help increase your abdominal strength. Work your way up to one minute for the front and thirty seconds for each side plank.

When doing exercise drills—including crunches or sit-ups—be sure to remember the orthopedic rule: "If you bend your back, you must also bend 'at least' one knee." That puts a new slant on lifting your clubs out of the trunk, doesn't it? Even if you bend a knee and lift one foot off the deck, your back is protected.

You don't need a gym or a lot of organization to do these plank exercises. And front or side, they won't hurt your shoulders.

Drill

Take an eight-pound medicine ball and throw it to a partner like a rugby pass—with the abdominal muscles fully
engaged. Use your thighs and gluteals for strength, and your
legs for turning the pass away to the waiting hands—as in
a golf swing. If you can't find a partner—then take a pillow
and pass it across the room into the far wall. That's what the
ninety-two-year-old friend of mine does. Not a bad looking
swing either.

Ninety-two-year-old Charles Hillman at Point Grey's 15th tee.

TIP 11

LATERALS, SHANKS, AND OTHER ANNOYING SELF-INFLICTED WOUNDS

No one wants to talk about shanks. In fact, lots of people will run if that most confidence-shattering stroke in golf is even mentioned. As a result, few know how to cure it. Let's take a look.

Shanks occur when, instead of hitting the ball on the center of the club's face, the golfer's hands move the hosel (the socket of a golf club head in which the shaft fits) closer to the side of the ball—they're only an inch and a half apart to begin with. You can close this distance and ruin your round in a number of ways:

- Ranked number one in the world standings, Lee Westwood blew a European Tour lead when he disconnected his right elbow from his hip reaching for the ball while coming down the stretch in the lead on the sixteenth hole in 2011.
- Johnny Miller shanked a seven iron on the fifteenth hole at Pebble Beach in a playoff with Jack Nicklaus, when a lateral slide sent his ball bounding down Seventeen Mile Drive.
- Ben Hogan shanked a five iron over some empty bleacher seats during a Monday morning practice round with three wide-eyed rookie pros. Hogan's caddie just dropped another ball and the game went on without any mention of the incident (what incident?).

The main cause of the dreaded lateral occurs when the golfer points the butt end of the grip to the "out-field"—over the far side of the target line—and the hosel moves an inch closer to the sweet spot on the ball. Once that "flop-over" happens, the golfer never really has a chance, because when the lead hand points palm-down to the ground, there just isn't much time to get the club head square to the target line again—like it was on the take-away.

This move of the left palm flopping over to face the grass is a double-cross because the golfer is trying to be "rhythmical" and perform the chip smoothly. Now the butt end of the grip is pointing across the target line into the outfield, and the golfer pulls the hosel into the back of the ball.

Cure: use Hogan's take-away, where the back of the left hand is angled to the ground along the target line. The knuckles of the left hand are looking downward because the hands don't move by themselves. They hold their molded position as they are pushed back along the target line by the left shoulder moving down.

The first stage of a take-away with eight iron.

Then, in the second stage of the take-away, the left wrist hinges. There is now a concave look to both hands and the palms face each other.

The second stage with hinging.

If you pause at this hinged position, you will notice that the club shaft, when it arrives at the horizon—as if for a long pitch—is parallel to the target line.

Pushing higher in the back swing—as needed for a strong "half shot"—the club's shaft is straight up in the air; the butt end of the grip is pointed at the infield grass.

The golfer's hands are not flopped over pointing to the outfield. Aim the butt end of the club's grip to the inside edge at the back of the ball. Raising your left shoulder will bring the right elbow to reconnection with the rib cage, and you're ready for the turn of the hips and the strike. Now you have some insight into why Mike Weir, the 2003 Master's champion, has a pre-swing routine which rehearses the first two take-away actions.

When one thinks about his pre-shot routine for a moment, it's pretty darned smart. It checks for a hand-angle which could cause a "flop-over." Instead, the golfer rehearses the "right" way. Taking those extra three seconds in a pre-shot routine are a lot better than figuring out the answer to, "Where the hell did that shank come from?"

Turning through the ball down the target line.

Drill

Address the ball with a long straight line from lead shoulder to club head. The left wrist should be flat. The right hand is in dorsiflexion, with a concave angle that does not change throughout the shot.

Hit twenty half shots with your eight iron with good first stage hand action on the take-away to the right knee area.

First stage of take-away with the palm of the right hand pointed squarely back at the ball.

Then hinge the wrist to waist height so that you can pause to check the position of the shaft and butt end of the grip at half way. The left wrist is in dorsiflexion (concave/cupped/collapsed) and so is the right hand. The palms of both hands face one another. The left palm is not turned down to the grass.

You will recall that in this half-way position, the timing for the strike is at a simple level. The lead shoulder rises, and the right knee, pulled by the rotating left hip, drives under the ball at the same time.

Let's add one special detail to develop a "knuckles down" punch shot.

Now raise the left shoulder so that the butt end of the club starts down to the back of the ball, arch the left hand, and twist the back of the hand toward the ball so that the knuckles turn toward the ground. Now hit the back of the ball with knuckles looking at the ground—just as they did on the first stage of the take-away.

You will hit the ball first with this shot—taking the divot after the ball—thus creating spin and a lower trajectory...as you might want to do as you perform a "punch shot" onto a firm green. In the photo below, please note that because of the twisting hand, the butt end of the grip is past the ball and still moving toward the target, but not flipping a collapsed wrist so that the grip moves in the opposite direction, away from the target.

Just before impact of the "knuckles down" punch shot. There could be a lot more lower body movement than in this photo. Check page 112 for Mr. Hogan's position.

Quick Review

How not to shank: For the take-away of a long chip, the right knee is pressed in toward the ball as if anticipating the impact position. The left-leading hand is twisted and arched into the exact position that you would like at impact. For the take-away, this flat (square) left wrist pushes away from the ball straight back along the target line until it reaches the stationary right knee. At this point the center of the right palm is aimed at the back of the ball.

Now here's a part that's a bit tricky to put into words: On the take-away, when the left hand reaches the right knee, the left wrist begins to hinge into a concave position called dorsiflexion, where the heel of the left hand is pushing down the toe line and away from the target. The left thumb turns up to point at the sky. Now both hands are in dorsiflexion, facing each other, with both thumbs pointing upward.

The left hand does *not* pronate or roll so that the left palm looks at the ground—a position which would put the butt of the club handle pointing out over the target line.

The end of the club's grip is pointing down the infield between the toe line and the target line—and the imaginary dot on the palm of the right hand is aimed at the imaginary dot on the back of the ball.

Hogan knuckles down on a five iron.

TIP 12

SWINGING THROUGH
THE IMPACT ZONE

Probably the most important thing to perform during the hit of the ball is to learn to "swing the handle" and not the club head. If you are lucky and/or clever, you will have learned to do this while putting. The lesson to be learned is: do not let the hand action change so that the butt end of the grip stops moving forward toward the target, but instead suddenly begins moving "away" from the target. This faulty move prevents a square hit and ruins direction plans. The butt end of the club's handle must lead the hands past the ball toward the chosen target. This tip is to remind you of the right track for the hands as they pass through the impact zone.

Note that the right hand is still in dorsiflexion even though arched down the shaft in a line with the club's face.

"Flipping" is an attempt to gain more distance through hand speed. Of course the source of effective speed is the power provided by the legs and torso. Hence Tiger's advice to juniors not to flip.

The effect of having the hands flip is to have the toe of the club head snap closed during contact and the ball can go just about anyplace.

When your hands are a "molded unit" with the left, or lead hand, strong and square to the target, and your right hand is held in arched dorsiflexion playing a "supportive role"—like Hogan's—and not "hitting at" the ball, you can at least influence where it is going. Stressing this hand position will send the club face through the contact zone held square to the target for a significant time, which will produce a well-hit ball. Also, because your hands are in control of the club, you will see that the shaft stays low and parallel to the target line.

The first picture is typical of a young player snapping his hands over. With a "flip" the club head moves significantly inward and upward from the target line. The grip's end has suddenly reversed its direction away from the target and given up control of the head of the club.

For the model with flipping hands. Compare the difference with the Hogan swing-through. The head of the flipped club is further away from the target line.

One way to learn how to avoid the hand-flipping fault is to experience the path of a controlled grip in slow motion as your piano teacher likely requested.

Set up in a squared stance with the grip handle pointing at your belt buckle. That right hand angle is not going to change.

At address the butt end is pointing to belt buckle.

After phase one the butt end is still pointing to belt buckle.

Phase two. The butt end is still pointing at target.

Chipping is a good way to ingrain this position where the butt of the grip goes down the infield strip of grass between the toe line and the target line—past the ball—and then as the body turns toward the target, the butt end of the grip is still moving toward the target.

The torso rotates to the target, and although the handle inevitably changes direction, it does so while moving toward the target. As a result, there is no sudden flipping change which would make it impossible for the club face to come through the impact zone under the golfer's control. Try this with a stick at home.

Turning the torso keeps the heel of the grip moving toward the target. Because of the left arm connection to the rib cage, the handle begins turning around the body, and is slow to reverse direction of the handle which has been aimed toward the target.

Completion of the turn and extension points to the target.

High finish with the molded hands still in control.

Arnold Palmer's finish with the molded hands clearly in control. Like wielding a two-handed broadsword rather than a one-handed rapier.

TIP 13

POWER THROUGH
THE IMPACT ZONE

PHOTO COURTESY OF JAY HEBERT

Ben Hogan in a strong bar-stool position weeks after capturing the U.S. Open, and just prior to winning the 1953 British Open for the first time. He was ready.

What creates power-swing speed when the hands enter the impact zone? I hope you've been turning up to the top of your backswing with "moderate" pace—to make certain that you have enough control to complete your backswing—because now things are about to speed up markedly.

It might surprise you—when you finally grasp the importance of the concept that the hands don't really do much during this important phase of your swing—in fact, it may be argued that the less the hands do, the better the swing.

If you are a young gymnast on the university team for the "rings" event, you might have enough strength to rely on your arms to produce the power for your swing. But if you are pretty much an ordinary person, you had best let your torso and the big muscles around your hips (the abdomen, derriere, and thighs) produce the power. Babe Didrikson Zaharias, one of the greatest athletes of the twentieth century—and a woman just under Hogan's size—told a group of women what to do about strength when playing at Shaughnessy Heights one summer's evening long ago: "Swing your hips, girls. Your arms don't have it."

It's the torso that provides the power. So, let your hands be a molded unit as part of the "connected" magical device used to guide the tail-end of the club's grip down from the top of the backswing by pointing to the infield strip of grass. Let the arm triangle that Hogan called his "Magical Device" bring the club's head—with speed—into the back of the ball. Here's how:

1. Set up in a squared stance with the grip handle pointing at your belt buckle. That right hand angle is not going to change.

2. When the molded hands arrive at the right knee on the down-swing, both knees continue to accelerate the counter-clockwise "grind" which will drive the belt buckle and the third button of your shirt toward the target with ever-increasing speed.

3. The hands as a tight molded unit grip the butt end of the club from the right knee to the left knee. During this high-speed trip, the right hand "is along for the ride." It does nothing but hang on in a strong position of dorsiflexion, waiting for the left hand to lead the way—just as any skilled tennis player will demonstrate to you when putting topspin onto a two-handed forehand shot down the line.

Model with tennis racquet for two-handed forehand topspin. Note the extra strength added by the right arm locked in supination.

4. In golf, the left hand holds the club handle firmly with the last three fingers which are "in charge" of the grip. Then as the butt end of the club leaves the right knee to move across the center of the stance toward the left knee, the leading left hand turns its knuckles down into the back of the ball. This sequence can be easily reviewed at home in a mirror.

Left hand begins to twist knuckles down.

Left hand twists downward for impact. Right hand keeps its angle.
Elbows face forward for strength.

5. The torso—attached to the triangle—above a very strong bar-stool position rotates the golfer's hips and knees through the impact zone—in sort of an accelerated grinding move. The belly button stays behind the ball as the hips rotate in a barrel—counterclockwise with speed. The center of the chest turns through the ball, and on down the target line.

6. This counterclockwise rotation within the impact zone is led by the left hip, over a flexed left knee, while turning away from the target line with speed as the belt buckle is brought around to face fully square to the target.

PHOTO COURTESY OF MIKE LILLY

Tiger with knuckles down. That tennis player must have known something. Tiger's right arm is also locked tightly for strength through the thick rough.

TIP 14

HANDS HINGING FOR THE PUNCH SHOT

I'll bet you remember Canadian Mike Weir, the 2004 winner of the Augusta National Championship. His fellow champions certainly remember his choice of the dinner menu traditionally selected by the new title holder. Mike chose: elk, wild boar, Arctic char, and Canadian beer.

A great many golf fans might also remember his distinctive warm-up waggle. Weir would take his club head back a foot or two on his Hogan-like take-away path, with the back of the lead hand angled to the ground; then he would check something...no one could tell what...then he would continue on the backswing until his arms were just above his waist. He'd check again. Then he'd get back to his position of address, and play away.

Many have tried to ask him just what he was doing—good luck with that. Weir plays his cards as close to this vest as did Hogan, but here's what his close friends speculate:

One fellow tour player said, "He's probably checking his plane." And this could be. He might be looking where that tail end of the club's handle is pointing—preferably down the infield to the inside edge of the ball.

Another ventured, "He might be getting the feel of hinging his wrists properly." And saying this, he demonstrated.

When the hands reach the knee which is farthest away from the target—Mike Weir is left handed so I can't say it properly—the wrists begin to "hinge" into the stage before a full "cocking" of both wrists for a full shot.

So, if you're swinging from the right hander's stance, it would read like this:

As the hands hinge above the right knee, both thumbs turn in front of the golfer's chest and point up to the sky, with both hands showing the beginning of dorsiflexion heading to a full concave position for both hands at the top of a full swing.

First stage take-away. Knuckles down on the lead hand.

Second stage with hinging. Shaft parallel to ground as well as to the target line.

Ideally, the golfer keeps thumbs and shaft pointing to the sky as the hands rise to the top of this swing.

Now the golfer's arm is parallel to the ground and target line.

At this point, if the golfer permits the palm of the lead hand to flop over and turn to face the ground, he or she is heading for big trouble getting that club face back squared to the target line at the ball.

On the way back down to the impact zone, the hands will return to the same old spot in front of the right knee.

Coming back to the impact zone, the golfer's hands prepare to change.

Now the back of the left hand can return to the position of facing down to the target line in a position the pros called "knuckles down." The twist of the left hand is "supported" by the left forearm being held in a locked position with the "dimple" on the inside of the left elbow pointing up to the sky and held throughout the shot by the forearm—turned away from the body's center, with the left forearm locked in supination.

Knuckles turning down.

With this concept, we are stepping very close to "Hogan's secret," which is fully explained later. Hogan teased people along when they asked him to tell his secret, because as Hogan emphasized to Stan Leonard, he wanted to be paid for what took him years of arduous work to define. So when asked about his secret, he would say, "It's right in front of you...if you know where to look...and don't forget the waggle. It's really important. Makes you relax."

Then he would make elaborate passes above the ball—rolling (pronating) the left wrist away from the ball—as he never did with his backswing for an actual stroke.

The left hand would, unnoticed, switch into dorsiflexion, and he would appear to pronate his right hand over the ball. He would repeat this move two or three times. But what was he really doing? He was unobtrusively practicing the action of his left hand into the ball prior to the real swing and the real stroke—much like the "knuckles down" move above. The way Hogan met the ball with his left hand was the essence of Hogan's secret: the action of his left hand twisting and arching into the ball at impact. This was combined with a left forearm "locked" in supination. We shall discuss this detailed nuance in Tip 18.

Left elbow dimple facing sky. Right hand in dorsiflexion as at address.

On the swing through for the "punch shot," the golfer's hands and club shaft are again parallel to the ground as well as the target line. Because of the nature of the punch shot, the follow-through is slightly abbreviated. The palm of the right hand still faces the target. The back of the right hand still holds its angle of dorsiflexion.

Swing through for the punch shot.

The punch shot maintains good accuracy even in the winds of Texas, and Hogan was a master. So was Floridian Paul Azinger, who said of his favorite shot, "I should use this shot every time. Just take two extra clubs and fire under the wind."

PHOTO COURTESY OF FIRST CUT GOLF

For the restricted swing of the punch shot, the highest point in the follow-through has the heel of the grip pointing to the ground and the golfer's right hand is still in dorsiflexion.

TIP 15

CONTROLLING THE FADE

If you slice, chances are that this pesky distance stealer is developed by the upper body initiating the move down from the top of the backswing. Unless the legs start first, the hands and right shoulder will come over top of the ball with the driver's club face open to the target line.

Go and see a teaching pro and turn that distance-eating slice into a controlled fade—a stroke which has more power and more distance than the usual left-to-right spinning ball. A controlled fade can be a very useful shot. An asset which takes away problems on the left side of the fairway—just ask Nicklaus, Trevino, or Singh about the effectiveness of a fade.

A fade would suit you much better than a slice and there is more than one way to perform it, and maybe it should begin with evaluation of your grip.

Whoever said, "Hold the club as if you had a bird in your hand," sadly misjudged the strength of ball strikers. Ben Crenshaw stated flatly that, "No one swung at a golf ball with more force or authority than Hogan. His hands were like a pair of vices."

For a power fade, Hogan's long left thumb points down the shaft to the club's head. This position weakens the grip to prevent the club's face from closing.

The first three fingers of both hands squeeze a strong unyielding control of the club. The thumb and forefinger can be less intense.

Ways to Develop a Left-to-Right Spin

1. A wipe shot: This shot was a favorite of Mark Calcavecchia when it came to a tight hole with problems left. He would aim down the left third of the fairway and after getting in the bar-stool position, would pull the torso through the ball with his left hip turning hard in counterclockwise rotation. His hands were held firmly in place through the ball. The club face—square to the target line—feels like it has "wiped" across the ball as it is pulled into the "infield." The resulting left-to-right spin brings the ball into the center of the fairway.

2. A swing shortened: On the tee of a finishing hole like the eighteenth at Pebble Beach, a lot of pros are on the verge of making some good money, with only one last obstacle in their way—the Pacific Ocean. If ever they needed a solid fade, now was the time. Some merely shorten their back-

swing so that their left shoulder would not reach the ball. The lead shoulder would stop four to six inches short. I'm no physicist, so for reasons unbeknownst to me, that ball which must not go left, will not go left, and cannot go left. But you sacrifice distance. The next model demonstrates the "short shoulder."

3. A controlled fade: During the 1950s and '60s in Vancouver, there were teaching pros who studied Hogan and taught at least "part" of his system— the part they could see. So they taught this method that some used effectively. It was called a "controlled cut" which has been recently re-visited by golfing analyst John Miller, demonstrated here by gifted amateur Bert Ticehurst.

Miller and the teaching pros studied Hogan's follow-through—the only part moving slowly enough for examination—and found that if the follow-through of the swing was completed with the left palm facing the target, then a controlled fade had occurred. It certainly was the opposite

of Arnold Palmer's finish, with the left palm looking back in Arnie's face. Palmer's club face looked ahead to the target. The opposite cut-action finished with the club face looking back down the target line.

4. Hogan's power fade: This shot of course was Hogan's "go to" specialty, and even though he played at five feet eight inches tall on top of 145 pounds, he remained one of the tour's long hitters. Of course distance was the most important difference between Hogan's power fade and the other methods of making the ball go left to right. The "cut" shots could not match the distance of the power fade because Hogan could "extend" his hands down the shaft, pointing the club head after the ball to the target. He kept the right arm connected to the rib cage. The right elbow could slide off the iliac crest, up and across the center of the body, still connected…and the "cut shooters" couldn't extend like that.

PHOTO COURTESY OF GETTY IMAGES

Hogan extending on swing-through. The right hand holds a slight dorsiflexion with a long strong arch to hold the shaft on a solid path to the target.

However, it was his accuracy that amazed his fellow competitors as well as the galleries. He could put that ball where he wanted it, and when. This confident accuracy, which the Scottish public discovered during the British Open at Carnoustie, was to be recognized by an admiring nation of golfers as "the greatness of his game."

Which way would Hogan go at Cypress Point? To the left, making it a dog-leg par four with driver and five iron? Or rather, a faded one iron between the grove of Cypress and the cliff's edge, followed by a pin-seeking eight iron for birdie? In his famous match he was partnered with his old caddie friend Byron Nelson, against two amateurs of the day, Harvie Ward and Ken Venturi. In a great struggle, told shot-by-shot in Mark Frost's book entitled simply *The Match*, Hogan shot a 63 for a course record this day, and the pros beat the amateurs by one stroke. Hogan birdied this 17th hole the hard way, by following the cliff's edge.

TIP 16

DRAWING THE BALL

PHOTO COURTESY OF JOHN RUSSELL

As a power hitter, John Russell won an enviable record of amateur championships living with the long draw, his left hand strong enough to withstand breaking down. You can see that his right hand has no dorsiflexion past impact.

A controlled draw is one of the most satisfying events in golf. It does have a dangerous side however.

Known for his power fade, Ben Hogan certainly knew how to draw a ball. For him it was a matter of "changing the chuck on the lever." Meaning that he would merely change the grip on his club from a weaker—long left thumb down the shaft pointing at the ball—to a "stronger" grip where the two Vs made by the thumb and forefinger both pointed to the right shoulder.

Sean O'Hair's "strong" grip for a draw at Thousand Oaks. The Vs of both combinations of thumb and forefinger point to the right shoulder.

When Hogan wanted to draw the ball with a moderate right to left spin, he held the club with a stronger grip. His leading elbow was held in the "normal" position with the inside dimple of the left elbow facing inward toward the center of the body. The prominent point of the elbow bone—the "olecranon"—points at the target when the golfer is contemplating a "draw."

Hogan would rely on his stable stance, with the center of his body pointing to the ball, and was careful to swing with a gradual increase in tempo with his molded hands. The left forearm was allowed to roll over with slow supination, because there were three controlling features to balance the danger of snapping the ball sharply left.

First, his right elbow remained connected with the right side all the way through the shot, even into extension down the target line.

Second, the left shoulder moved straight up toward the left ear so that there is no shoulder movement pulling left away from the target line.

Third, the belly button and hips never stopped. They led the hands right through the shot.

These three checks and balances are safety features built into the swing to produce a controlled draw. Fred Couples, when asked about how he produced a draw, offered this thought: "I just think about it." With all those masterful years of experience behind him, no doubt he has ingrained the swing points to be reviewed before applying the image he is thinking about. Likely, he also has a clear image of the role of the contacting sweet spots as a guiding swing thought, and he puts them on the right collision course.

Somewhere in between Couples' thinking method and Nicklaus' grip reliance for drawing the ball stood Moe Norman. Moe would challenge the gallery watching him hit balls

Nicklaus at Whistler, getting ready to squeeze the "hell" out of his right hand.

to call out what they wanted in mid swing—and he could produce—proving that he had it all figured out and that he could change his hand action in mid swing. Not advised for everyone—unless you're hitting over one thousand balls per day.

Jack Nicklaus told the gallery how to draw the ball "quick and neat" at the Whistler Ski and Golf Resort, as he opened the majestic new "Nicklaus North" course that he designed for Vancouver golfer Caleb Chan. At the golf demonstration he offered up the mechanical explanation of how he performs his draw, as follows:

1. Don't change the swing at all.
2. Set up aiming your shoulder line to the right side of the target.
3. Aim the club face straight down the target line to the target.
4. Keep your tempo smooth.
5. Don't move your right hand—keep it strong and supporting.

Then Nicklaus looked with an "evil" grin at the caddie, who had been successfully—and at some times dramatically—stopping the new Titleist practice balls from rolling into a glacial river at the far end of the driving range. "Let's see if he stops this one," Nicklaus whispered to the gallery, just before he launched one of those "controlled satisfying events" that we all strive to perform.

Jason Day stretches down the target line. Compare his belt angle with the angle across his shoulders and you will see clearly that the bottom part of his body is separated from the top, because the legs and hips are ahead and more parallel to the ground than the two shoulders which operate more on a vertical plane. The right hand still holds hard to some of its dorsiflexion as it arches down the line and the right bicep is still glued to his chest. The divot indicates the ball's right-to-left spin.

TIP 17

PUTT FOR DOUGH

Ben Crenshaw, one of the great putters of the game, at Augusta National where he was twice a champion in 1984 and 1995. He demonstrates the useful mold of his hands.

Reluctantly leaving Pebble Beach and the Crosby National Pro-Am from the Monterey Airport, I climbed aboard the commuter plane for San Francisco International with two seats to choose from. I sat by the window, and was pleasantly surprised when Ben Crenshaw sat down next to me. Across the aisle from him was Andy Williams, TV host and singer of *Moon River* fame. They began to talk, so I just sat there beside one of the most skilled putters ever in the game of golf—because that's what the singer wanted to talk about—and Crenshaw was in great form.

Answering Williams' questions, Crenshaw spoke in glowing terms about some of golf's great putters and quickly sketched the talents of men like Bobby Locke of South Africa, who "hooked" his putts; Billy Casper who tried a similar overspin tactic; Bobby Jones and his putter "Calamity Jane"; and the studious Jack Nicklaus.

Leaving himself out of the list, Crenshaw turned his attention to fellow Texan Ben Hogan and began a description of an ability that was a complete surprise to me, and so speaking for the first time, I asked, "Hogan must have been a good putter. But was he great?"

Crenshaw responded quickly. "He was before that damned bus ran into him. Cut his left eye. Depth perception restricted. Ask yourself, how can a man go through major events like the Master's and U.S. Open—through all four rounds—and not have a three-putt? He was better than great."

The focus of the discussion for the remainder of the forty-minute trip was about Ben Hogan's putting and the details that went into it.

Key points in Hogan's detailed approach to putting:

A. When you want to practice your putting, do it without distractions. For example, when you want to drill with several balls, or warm up before a club tournament, get off to the far side of the green where you won't be in the way of others, and they won't interfere with you. There you can concentrate on the "feel" of the process, as well as the texture of the grass. Take a tee and plug it in off to the side, and away from the nine holes on the putting green.

B. Don't putt at a hole when you're going to hit several balls with a view to repeating the skill to be "memorized." You're not keeping score now. You should be concentrating on technique. You'll never have this exact putt ever again. Besides, when hitting one ball after another at a cup, have you ever kept track of how many practice putts go in? Not many. For longer putts, probably around 10 percent. Which leaves a very large percentage to destroy your confidence. You are supposed to be "drilling" and ingraining technique.

C. Use three balls for drills, and your concentration improves. Putt six-footers to a tee, and your learning, as well as your confidence, will increase. When out on the course you can imagine a tee on the edge of the cup right in line with the break of the green. You can visualize that all you have to do is roll the ball over that tee. Better yet, choose an intermediary target on the high point of the break—a blemish or a colored spot—from which the ball will roll into the center of the cup after running over this mark—like a skier's fall-line.

D. After a drill session to a tee peg, you might want to test yourself using the regular cup. This can be beneficial. However, you are allowed but "one ball" over nine holes, and as in competition, you putt out each hole. Preferably, you will play a money game with a buddy to test your prowess while keeping it strictly to the rules of golf. As an aside: you might not know that there is a game for patios overlooking the eighteenth green. They throw a dollar into a pot. Look down the fairway and pick a golfer from the next foursome by shirt color, and watch—that's your bet.

The first ball to "go in the hole" wins the pot. You'll be amazed at how few balls get there. If you ever hear cursing from the patio, you'll know that someone on the green just knocked away another two-footer as a "gimme" and the pot was lost. But back to our discussion.

Michelle Wie is a Stanford graduate, a beautiful young woman, and one hell of a golfer.

Going through a putting slump, Michelle has taken some of Hogan's techniques to get back where she belongs on the leader board. She has both of my Hogan books and hopefully they will suggest some point which will help her perform to the levels indicated by her tremendous talent. I first met Michelle with her father and mother at Vancouver Golf Club for the 2012 Canadian Open for women.

She hit full shots that any golfer would envy, but putting let her down. Following an opening round in the mid-seventies it appeared unlikely that she would duplicate her impressive three-stroke victory at the 2010 Canadian Open at St. Charles in Winnipeg with a total score of twelve under par. This win added nicely to her present-day $3 million in prize money.

Following her frustrating round, she joined the crowd of LPGA players who were all very intent on the putting process. They crept around as if on thin ice, and as if the ball were a hand grenade. The exception was Michelle, who was very businesslike for thirty minutes or more, putting in a style reminiscent of George Knudson, and showing indications as to a likely cause for her undeserved high number of putts per round. The "low left hand" on the grip appeared to be responsible for an extremely high follow-through—not at all like the "long and low" forward swing that Ben Hogan strived for.

Wie's high follow-through while putting.

Ben Hogan putting at Winged Foot in the 1959 U.S. Open. Note the low follow-through with the club's face square to the target, as it was at address.

The last thing to do before walking to the first tee is to putt three balls downhill to a peg six feet away. Then three more uphill, and get each putt a foot past the tee. This is your day.

Putting to a tee peg. Review your five pre-shot routine: ball position, grip, connection points, hover, photo of ball's path. You're ready.

TIP 18

HOGAN'S SECRET—WHEN YOU'RE READY

Before you begin this section, may I suggest respectfully that you wait until you've been successful with several of the earlier tips? I've been slipping you little parts of the large Hogan system, in staircase fashion, to prepare you for the last step—the nucleus of his swing secret.

You should be prepared to follow his formula, which is thirty repetitions per day for seven days. Then you'll have it. From then on it requires only daily visits of three or four reps. If you do it, you'll never regret that first week at fifteen minutes per day given over to ingraining this skill.

Ben Hogan had a secret, but because cameras in the mid twentieth century did not have the lens speed for the job, no one could actually see the action of his hands in the photo. Further, Hogan was not eager to tell the truth about what had taken him so long to learn. He emphasized to Stan Leonard, "Make 'em pay for your hard work."

Later, in his famous book *Five Lessons*, Mr. Hogan used terms like "supination" and "pronation" that he learned from the gifted Anthony Ravielli, his medical journal artist who did not play much golf. Hogan was not all that fluent with anatomical terms. The result? Chaos. With tongue in cheek, teaching pros said that they were most appreciative for the book because it made them a great deal of money...trying to repair damage done by the misinformation.

The real secret? They could only guess. As a result, there developed more than fifty years of speculation as to what went on in the impact zone. We have saved the discussion of Hogan's secret until the last tip, only if you feel up to it, because it will take a bit of time that might not be available to you.

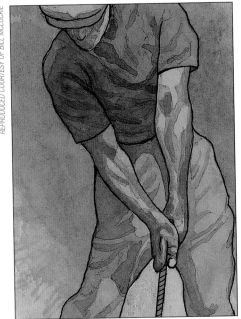

Note the added structural support for the hands at impact by the elbows turned skyward and locked into position. Both arms pressed into the rib cage. Hands arched toward the ball. What could break down?

A full shot with a long shaft requires strong support. Hogan's arms are connected to the torso, with the elbows locked in position, and the left elbow "dimple" pointing to the sky. He recommended that the right elbow be held the same way, and I notice that Tiger does this at times. The arms are firmly connected to the rib cage, then the torso rotates with power. Only the left hand moves by itself during the last foot or so of the impact zone. And practicing just this little move during pitching drills with half shots is very enlightening. You'll hear a different click-sound with a different solid feel. It's one of the reasons prompting Ben Crenshaw to state that, "Hogan was a master at pitching."

Now that you've gone through some of the tips that you may not have known or tried before, let's end with the "biggie": Hogan's secret. This action may not be for everyone. It's a simple move—undetectable by onlookers—however, the positioning and timing of his secret, with the other coordinating body parts, demands some "drilling" time. You see, Hogan's secret is not just a flip of a switch, it's part of a system which is interdependent. Like a spider's web, it's a system that touches every club—with the exception of the right-hand bunker explosion shot.

The essence of the secret is the part that even experts couldn't see—the left hand movement. And the part they could see—the right hand—they didn't believe.

Golfers did not accept that the right hand "did nothing." After all, Hogan had said—in an attempt to throw off a persistent inquirer probing for his secret—"I wish I had two right hands to hit the ball with." (Later, he upped it to "three.") Further, they recalled their robust Cro-Magnon days when one whack with a strong right hand was good enough to "bring home dinner." But the modern reality was that the right hand was just along for the ride while trying to support the left hand during its move into the golf ball.

For good golf, the right hand is a "supporting hand." Its only movement is to arch, and add strength to the molded hand-set ready for impact. And it is for this crucial instant we can understand Stan Leonard's observation that the grip is like "wringing a towel" with both palms squeezing as if trying to turn to the sky.

The right hand keeps its dorsiflexion well past impact, and even throughout a long extension of the shaft and arms.

The part they could not see was the action of the left hand as it came into impact. Here the left hand clenches the last three fingers into its own palm (palmar flexion) and squeezes tight. While this palmar flexion occurs, there begins an arching of the left hand, and both hands push their thumbs arching down at the ball. This arching creates a spine for the added strength needed to withstand the force of the hit. And strength prevents the collapse of the left wrist during impact. Look again at Hogan's serial representation of the action of the left hand through the impact zone. We could, I believe, add even more "arch" to the left-hand sketch as it approaches the ball. Check again the previous painting of Hogan's hands at impact.

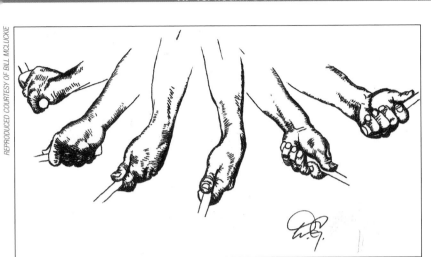

For a power fade the left forearm is locked in supination throughout the swing. This control procedure prevents the forearm from rolling over toward the target, a move which would change the club's face, ideally held open one or two degrees to deny the hook, and promote the fade.

Hogan hated a hook, saying, "It's like a rattlesnake in your pocket." So he won everything in the golf world by developing a power fade, his "go to" shot for good length, but above all, accuracy. As Tiger Woods acknowledged: "Ben Hogan was the best driver of the golf ball there ever was." And Jack Nicklaus responded in kind: "Hogan was the greatest shot maker I ever saw."

Hogan was able to win these accolades from fellow top echelon champions because of the following action: both hands approach the ball in dorsiflexion, but the left hand anticipates the hit, and twists the leading wrist so that the back of the hand is in a "high" arch, and this strongly held arch flattens the lead wrist into a very strong lever which brings the unrelenting club head into the heart of the ball.

No matter what some interpreters say, the left hand does not supinate into impact. The correct move is a "palmar flexion" (like making a flat-wristed fist). And while the palmar flexion is being made, the wrist arches and holds tight for the shock of impact. The forearm is held locked in supination throughout the swing, and does not "roll over" toward the target. The right hand squeezes the last three fingers strongly and arches down toward the ball. This action is mutually supportive, and creates an unyielding, molded unit for impact.

The only hand that makes a move is the left hand as it twists from dorsiflexion to palmar flexion with a strong grip on the last three fingers. The timing for the left hand's twist is just as the butt of the grip comes to the ball.

If you can get the feel of this position and its movement, you will be able to control the ball's direction rather than the same old "crap-shoot." And the best way to get the timing of all these subtle moves in synch is to hit thirty pitches for seven days. This drill will give you greater control and make you a golfer.

Warning: when your perfectly natural urge to try this with your driver comes to mind, smother it! Stay with the daily drill with your pitching wedge for one week. Feel the solid hit with the knuckles down, and the triangle connected. Count the sharp clicks. Then after seven days, try Hogan's secret with the driver. If it were as easy as you assumed, wouldn't everyone be doing it by now? The truth is that someone gets keen, may even try it for a few shots before grabbing a driver, becomes frustrated, skips the next day because of an appointment, tries a few shots the following day, stops after nine range balls, then gives up because "it doesn't feel right." Or: "It doesn't work for me."

Nevertheless, when all the arguments are done, there is now a definition of Ben Hogan's secret that we can use as a reference to our attempts:

When Hogan's secret is applied, the left forearm is held in "locked supination" with the upper arms of the Magical Device still strongly connected to the torso. This connected partnership prevents the left forearm from rolling over as molded hands approach the ball.

Now the secret is applied as the left hand twists into palmar flexion while the right hand maintains its dorsiflexion throughout the hit.

Both hands, however, arch their thumbs toward the ball, and we see the value in Moe Norman's description of Hogan's procedure as "Twist and Arch."

In a nut shell the definition can be summed up as:

Hogan's secret is the palmar rotation and arching of the lead hand at impact.

And so, one thing is now obvious: Hogan was correct when he stated, "It's easy to see when you know where to look."

Hogan's molded grip—"like two vices," Crenshaw said.

For a power fade, what really separates Hogan's "secret move" above all other techniques to guarantee a "can't-go-left shot" is captured in the next photo of this superb athlete in action. Hogan is extending through impact with a four wood, with both hands in a mold swinging down the target line. Other methods to produce a left-to-right spin "hold off" with a slightly abbreviated swing, thus reducing distance. Hogan has reached to the limit here, and yet his right hand still holds a diminished dorsiflexion while both hands stretch to a full arch.

PHOTO COURTESY OF JULES ALEXANDER

Pure Hogan

Ben Hogan was a champion golfer who walked in quiet dignity through the privacy of his own world. Protected by insular mannerisms, he confused most people about his inner thoughts to the point where they came to believe that he was somehow devoid of feelings. However, caddies close to him knew that golf's fans did not see the man who helped those who needed the break he never had. He'd look after them, like the young pro who arrived at Colonial Club for an assistant's job without a jacket for the interview. Mr. Hogan gave him his. Or the Shady Oak Country club's staff when Hogan was adopted by a stray dog called "Buster." He paid for the care of this dog that sat in the cart watching him practice, and he cried like a wounded kid when Buster passed away.

Born into the poverty which drove his blacksmith father to commit suicide in front of him, nine-year-old "Bennie" helped his mother hold the family together by caddying and selling newspapers. School became a distant second choice. Looking back at what motivated him, Hogan stated: "I didn't want to be a burden to my mother. I needed to put food on the table. I needed a place to sleep."

Small in stature, Ben became a professional golfer who, with a terrible hook, tried to eke out a living on the struggling "PGA Gold Trail." When reduced to living on stolen oranges from the orchards of California, he was forced to return home to Texas for some form of work to gather enough money to try again. "My greatest accomplishment," he would come to say, "was being able to make a living playing golf after twice going broke."

His peers remembered him as the man who invented practice, because when Hogan's obsession with practice helped him to define his complex swing style, he climbed to the top of the PGA scoreboard as the best of the best. He won everything in America. He had reached the summit. And then, when driving home in winter fog on February 2, 1949, he was met head-on by a bus, driven by a substitute driver, passing a car on a bridge at fifty miles per hour. He barely survived.

Following more than one year of agonizing rehabilitation, Mr. Hogan began to climb the mountain again. He didn't stop until he had won five of the six tournaments he entered. He lost in his first competition—the Los Angeles Open—losing a playoff to Sam Snead.

"My legs hurt like Hell," Hogan remembered. He then won the unprecedented "Hogan Slam" of professional golf in 1953: the Master's, the U.S. Open, and the British Open for what has been called the greatest comeback in the history of sport.

When the pain of his shattered body reduced his game to levels with which he could not compete as he wanted to, he retired to make top quality golf equipment as he watched the years unfold. Some of his later reflections on the game leave us with thoughts to savor, and to consider well, such as those in the comprehensive work by Rich Skyzinski entitled *Quotable Hogan*, a text which sweeps across every stage of the Hawk's remarkable career.

Concerning practice, Hogan knew that this work had taken him years to shed his caddie swing with its vicious hook. He practiced with a purpose in mind for every shot he hit. Every shot was aimed at a target, then he studied the flight of the ball . . . and he learned.

Socially, Hogan was his own worst critic and realized that he was on a lonely road. There was his true love, Valerie of course, and a few trusted friends, but he was often curt with people. One of his Shady Oak caddies told me: "Mr. Hogan didn't like to chat. He just wanted to play golf."

However, there was one member at Shady Oaks who came to know a different side of Mr. Hogan. Kris Tschetter was in her first year at Texas Christian University and the reigning 1983 American Junior Golf Association Champion who, as a budding amateur, had her sights on becoming an LPGA professional. Members at Shady Oaks were requested "not to bother Mr. Hogan," and so despite a natural friendliness prompting a greeting for everyone, she pretended not to notice him. Soon tiring of this facade, she bade him "good morning" and was pleasantly surprised. Hogan answered back. It seems he had been impressed with the diligence of her practice regime, and quietly offered to help—if Kris needed it. A life-long friendship began.

As the years passed, Kris joined the women's tour in 1988 at age twenty-four and won the Northgate Classic, and was runner up in the 1996 U.S. Women's Open. More and more she began to share informal moments with Hogan on subjects far removed from golf. They were friends, and she wrote a book about her friend, with the title *Mr. Hogan, The Man I Knew*.

Interviewed by *Golf Digest* on video, she tried to let the fans know what he was really like. "Mr. Hogan had an amazing heart. He always noticed the underdog and tried to help them. Of course, he never wanted anyone to know!"

Kris believed that people would enjoy seeing him as she did. "I just liked him as a person. He had a great sense of humor and he would have me laughing every day when we hit balls. We would talk about so much more than golf. He kept people at a distance because he didn't really trust their motives. They were interested in Ben Hogan the golfer. I was interested in Ben Hogan the man."

Another golfer, Sergeant Tim Mincarelli, was also interested in Hogan's withdrawn manner. He was with the U.S. Marine Corp in Vietnam 1967–68 as one of those making a last stand at Khe Sanh in the seventy-seven-day siege. Wounded, he was to develop Post Traumatic Stress Disorder and felt that he understood Hogan's personality completely.

"Seeing his father die like he did brings on a lifetime of PTSD. If it is allowed to go unchecked you become a guy like he was. In many ways I am like him: I like to be alone, hate small talk, I would rather hit balls by myself all day than play, can't stand to play with high handicappers. I'm the guy sitting alone at the coffee shop in a golf hat watching everyone sit together in circles, laughing and talking about nothing."

Stan Leonard was one of the few lucky tour pros who were invited to play practice rounds with the distant Ben Hogan. During these moments, he was privy to Hogan's strategy for playing the game strategically. He played each hole with his target as the center of the green. With that in mind, he then tried to turn the ball toward the pin when it was on one side or the other. When the pin was at the front, he played it in high. If at the back, the ball went in low and rolling.

Leonard was advised that Hogan's general strategy was to play the hole the safest and easiest way to get the score you want, because as *Quotable Hogan* noted, "Golf is a game of misses. And the guy who makes the best misses wins."

This lesson was brought home during Stan's first round at the Colonial in Fort Worth. "I'll show you the course," Hogan said as they teed it up for the first hole, a 565-yard par five with two bunkers in front of the green with a narrow strip of fairway leading to the flag.

Stan outdrove Hogan and both were down the middle. Hogan played his second shot short of the bunkers with a direct angle to the pin.

Stan hit his second shot on the screws and the ball rolled up the strip of grass between the two bunkers and onto the far away green. It was a majestic shot which ran right at the hole and . . . mercy . . . lipped out . . . just missing golf's ultimate shot—a double eagle for three under par!

The fans whooped and hollered then applauded as Hogan's third shot with a pitching wedge finished two feet from the cup for a tap-in birdie four.

Stan lined up his eight-foot putt for eagle but missed, and wrote down four on his card. Hogan gave his friend a smile, "Nice birdie for the tie, Stan. If you'd have hit one of those bunkers I might be one up."

Ben Hogan discovered and created a "system" for golf which some say is the closest to perfection as anyone is going to get. It worked, and it was stunning to watch, even the sound of his club face colliding with the ball was sharp and alarming. But would it last?

I heard my favorite Hogan story from Mike Wright, the head professional at Shady Oaks in Westworth Village, Texas. He is very likely the last person to see Ben Hogan strike a golf ball. At age eighty, we can suppose that this proud champion wondered if the system he spent so long developing still worked, and so he surprised Mike by showing up at the pro shop one day when few people were around.

Hogan asked for his driver and three balls, then went out to the tenth tee where a par four dog-leg hole lay empty. Mike obliged, and watched from the shop window as the Hawk set it up. The hole was 370 yards long and well trapped. To open the green to the best angle for a tucked left pin, the drive should be to the right of center and past the fairway traps. Mr. Hogan hit three balls with his signature power fade, smiling and nodding as they all came to rest near each other in the preferred spot.

Mr. Hogan returned to the shop where he handed in his club, thanked the pro with a wave, then left the game forever, passing away in 1997 at the age of eighty-five.

Venturi said it for a lot of Hogan's friends: "A talent like this should live forever."

EPILOGUE

We get a hard look at ourselves through golf. Philosophers will tell you there are two main constants through life. One is the inevitability of death; the other is the inevitability of change.

As one ancient philosopher pointed out: the same man does not walk through the same river twice—the man changes the river and vice versa. What this means to you, in golf, is the penetrating observation by Stan Leonard that "a good swing is destroyed a millimeter at a time." This observation means that when swinging well, confidence tempts one to try to get a little bit more distance, or spin, or draw, or height, and the swing changes ever so slightly, and it keeps changing until the whole thing is out of whack.

Trust me, this will happen to you over and over again. "I haven't sunk a putt in a week!" So what do you do? The answer is clear. Go back to square one—check Hogan's instruction, and use his formula again: thirty repetitions per day for seven days.

And then check your alignment diagram before each shot: steps 1, 2, 3, 4, 5, until they become automatic again.

1. Place the leading foot on your chosen spot.
2. Squeeze the three fingers of the lead hand like Hogan.
3. Connect the arm and shoulder triangle to the torso.
4. Hover the club by arching the shoulder tips up and back.
5. Take a mental photograph of your target, then swing the club down that line.

APPENDICES

Quick Fixes for the 19th Hole

A. When you're under a tree and you "must not" go left, take out your driver and if you have a decent lie, give it a smooth swing. The ball will go low under the branches, slowly bending to the right, away from any trouble on the left—guaranteed. Quick story: Lanny Wadkins won the PGA championships on Sunday, August 14, 1959, and wanted to reap the benefits, but he had an appointment for a corporate breakfast and exhibition round at Point Grey Golf Club in Vancouver 9 o'clock a.m. Monday morning. Naturally, with better offers, Lanny wanted to skip this business deal but the chairman said, "No way. You've got a contract for $1,500. Be there!"

   So, sure enough, Lanny showed up for breakfast and a few words of welcome, then out he went—no warm-up, no measurement book—just straight to the tee and off he went, followed by a hundred spectators including me. Nothing unusual happened until the fifteenth tee to a slight dog's-leg right four par, narrowed by plenty of tree trouble and OB on the left side.

Lanny had a quick look, turned the driver's head backwards, and smacked the leading edge of the face into the ground, just hard enough to bring up a little ridge of grass. He placed his ball on the ridge—no tee—then lashed a low and controlled slider down the center.

He shot a very tidy sixty-eight that day, collected his $1,500 check, and left. In the parking lot before getting into a waiting car, he responded to my question about fifteen tee, and answered succinctly: "No one can hit a driver left from off the deck. No one."

B. Jack Nicklaus, the man to beat for thirty years, added a clever variation to his practice regime by taking only two clubs: the one he liked best, and the club he had the most trouble with. He would hit one hundred balls alternating these two clubs between each shot until he felt comfortable with both.

C. The tennis racquet represents a club face coming into impact. You will notice that the grip is "strong" with the lead hand in "slight pronation" and that the point of the left elbow is pointed at the target. This position gives a significant angle to the face of the hitting instrument—be it a golf club, tennis racquet, or ping pong paddle. The rotation of the left forearm will promote the right-to-left spin of a draw.

D. This tennis racquet shows that the angle of the face of the "hitting instrument" has decreased to two or three degrees because the left arm is locked in supination. The arms are strongly connected to the upper body "triangle." Turning the body through impact will develop the power fade because the slight angle of the face is held constant.

E. Chipping tip: short chips use exactly the same technique as a putt. The address position for the body is as close to the impact position as possible: weight on lead foot; hips rotated toward the target; hands arched and twisted for impact; right knee unmoving and flexed. Just like a twenty-foot putt. The tempo is slow during the short backswing, and slightly accelerated for the longer through-swing. Don't worry about hitting it too hard. Try this rhythm ten times and you'll see that it's the length of backswing that determines the distance the ball will roll, so it doesn't matter how far toward the target that you extend the club face. Distance has already been established by the backswing, but some golfers hear an inner voice saying, "Not too far!" and invariably they decelerate into impact with the ball—short again. They might blame the "damned greens" but it's really them—not going through the ball toward the target.

F. The good news about these tips is that they work as long as you don't start adjusting them to some new insight into the laws of applied physics that you will no doubt hear about, or imagine for yourself. The bad news is that the memory of execution will inevitably diminish because of the main law of the universe—things change.

For example, when the "timing" of your swing disappears on you—likely because of lack of practice—don't worry; you're only human, after all. I believe it was Jan Paderewski, the great pianist who said, "If I miss practice one day I know it. After two days the critics know. Three days and the public can tell." So, just go back to "square one" and review the details in front of a mirror.

G. When you release your right side for the "hit," make sure all the parts that make up the "right side" come down the infield and "under" the ball. Led by the right knee, the right shoulder and right hip follow a path down the infield—under your chin toward the target. Practice the "feel" of this in front of a mirror. Mark in your mind that position of the left shoulder at the top of the backswing. The right shoulder must *pass under* this spot in order to avoid swinging the right shoulder *over the top* of the ball.

Imagine a line drawn across Jason Day's shoulders and one across his belt line to see the separation he has created between upper and lower body. They should not move together. The leading left hip is clearing out of the way on a circular path. The tips of both shoulders are tilting down and up like a teeter-totter. (Yes, you've seen this photo before, on page 143. But it's worth repeating.)

H. Coming down from the top requires "sitting on the bar stool" and then separating the top half of the body from the bottom half. Below is an email to a friend about the frustrating necessity of learning a left-brain analysis for a right-brain vision. I was trying to convince him that you have to wrestle with memorizing the sequence—in front of a mirror preferably—and make it your own. Then you will develop top-level timing leading to a more powerful swing:

Just starting down, your club shaft has a very good plane in relation to the ball. The grip end is pointed at the back of the golf ball, and not pointed way over into the "outfield" toward the tray of balls.

However, your elevated right heel indicates that you do not have the correct "timing" for bringing the club down to the entrance of the impact zone.

You're missing the first move down, which is to "sit on the bar stool" by moving your left knee into position and "settling" into that strong position where your knees will drive the hips into impact by means of a rotation "within the barrel." The hands are to be moved by tilting shoulders.

The left knee moves first, back to its address position. Then the right knee waits for a split second (for what?, you ask) for the left shoulder to rise, which will put the right elbow back on the right rib cage. Then you're ready to release the right side.

Here is Luke Donald in the classic, athletic, strong power position, beginning to rotate the hand mold which is about to re-connect to the right side by squeezing the right elbow or bicep to the rib cage.

I. You should never "flip" your hands by collapsing the lead wrist, overpowered by the trailing hand which should remain in dorsiflexion. A flip is counterproductive because of the "great" change in position of the club face in relation to the target line. You can see by the following photos that the club head level—my grandson's putter—is six rock levels (about one foot) higher when the hands are flipped.

This is a short club. A regular length shaft changes the position of the club face by over two feet. The flip would open a wide range of possible directions somewhere between the extended angle of the shafts. The flip extends well to the left of the target line, and Hogan's extension remains on the target line.

J. There is a "point of balance" that is very rewarding to "feel" every once in a while. It is a place in the impact zone where the club seems to lose its weight, and it becomes very easy to turn the butt end of the club handle from its aim at the flag, to being pointed into the belt buckle as the club's head now aims at the target. This is good for mirror work. You find this balance point by assuming the "bar-stool" position, then holding the right angle between the left arm and the shaft while turning the connected torso to face the target. The butt end of the grip in your hand mold moves across to the left knee. It is then that the body turns the triangle toward the target.

Bar stool

Point of balance

Hands to target

K. When playing a ball out of the rough, as in a sand bunker, make sure you open the blade so that when the grass catches the leading hosel it twists the face into the direction of the target instead of yanking it far left—as a square address would produce. It also helps to pick the club face up steeply with the hands as in a bunker. There is no need for any extension away from the ball on the take-away.

Final Quiz

Quick questions you should now be able to answer:

1. From the top of the backswing, what is the first move down?

   During a full take-away, the left knee is pulled inward toward the center of the stance. Once the hands come near to the top, the knee moves back over the flat left shoe—as it was at address—and this move is the beginning of a counter-clockwise rotation of the hips. This hip action separates the lower half of the body from the upper body, and also signals the left shoulder to rise straight up to the sky, parallel to the target line. This rise tilts the triangle so that the right elbow reconnects with the right side of the torso. And now the lower body rotates with increasing speed through the impact zone.

2. What is the action of the back knee?

The right knee remains flexed and slightly "kicked in" with the weight on the inside edge of the shoe. (The first tip I got from Dick Zokol was: "Never let the weight of the right knee get outside on the little toe.")

3. When does the lead knee straighten?

The lead knee straightens long after the ball is in flight, and the right side has turned through the shot so that the belt buckle is facing the target and the right toe is balancing the full follow-through.

4. How do you connect the arms to the torso?

The arms are connected to the rib cage by pressing the armpits to the body. The right elbow is resting near the iliac crest, and as the club head swings through the golf ball for a full shot, the elbow is "dragged" across the lower torso, still connected, but pulled away from the pelvic crest by the rotating hips.

5. What are the three benefits of hovering the club at address?

    a. You can relax your "big" muscle groups before twisting them to their fullest as when driving. The handle is held firmly by the last three fingers of the left hand, but the arms and shoulders, although connected, are relaxed.

    b. There is nothing to take the club face off line—such as pulling in or flicking out—and you won't catch the club head on long grass.

    c. The most important benefit from hovering is a take-away with tempo—slow and smooth—so that you can complete the backswing.

6. How can you practice effectively every day?

Whenever you can find ten minutes, take a small vacation and do some mirror work, or stroke six-foot putts at a dime on the carpet, or chip down a hall carpet while focusing on keeping the butt end of the grip in front of the ball.

7. What are the five navigator's "check points" before each shot?

    a. Position the ball in your stance.

    b. Form the hands into the impact mold.

    c. Check your connection points: both arms to shoulders, and the right elbow to the hip.

    d. Arch back the shoulder tips to hover the putter.

    e. Take a picture of the target—hold it as an image, and stroke to it.

8. What is the easiest and most surefire way to improve your golf score?

Start taking a bottle of water in your bag and have a drink every hole. Then stop at every water fountain and refill. I kid you not. If you stay hydrated you will gain the following advantages: sustained energy; improved concentration; and strength for the entire eighteen holes.

9. What about moderate daily exercise?

You've certainly heard this admonishment before, but consider for just a moment what it would be like if you actually did exercise every day? Increased libido, greater strength, less risk of diabetes, heart attack, or stroke, and more flexibility. These outcomes are all well and good I suppose, but when we're looking at knocking five points off your handicap rating, exercise might become a serious consideration for you.

Good luck to all. This game is worth the effort.

ACKNOWLEDGMENTS

Near the end of his career, Ben Hogan said, "I would like to be known as a gentleman first, and next as a golfer" and perhaps this statement goes a long way in explaining why he felt so strongly about Jim Langley, the beloved professional at Cypress Point Club. It became easily apparent that these two remarkable men shared so many of the values attributed to gentlemen, quite apart from their ability to play the game.

Born July 21, 1937, Jim passed from the company of his admiring and famous friends on July 20, 2013, just one day before his seventy-sixth birthday. A humble and courteous man, Jim was put in charge of one of the most treasured courses on earth, by way of hard work—the rough but common American road to one's dreams. He studied at the University of California in Berkeley where he met his "true love" Louetta, as she cheered his Golden Bears on to a National Basketball championship in 1959. After graduation, they married, and Jim had a short term as a PGA Tour player, but when his family grew, with two-year-old Brad and one-year-old Brett in tow, Jim predictably chose family first over golf, and joined his father's packing plant in Salinas, just as in *East of Eden*. Someone must have recognized the powerful character traits that Jim possessed, because he was hired for the dream job as head professional at Cypress Point, the "Sistine Chapel of Golf." Here, Jim shares the course record of sixty-three, with good friend Ben Hogan.

Following a thirty-four-year tenure at Cypress Point Club, Jim retired in 2006, but was immediately given an honorary membership—the club's second such honor, following Dwight D. Eisenhower, the thirty-fourth President of the United States. He continued playing with members even after being victimized by an accident which all but destroyed the function of his right arm. Just a few years before retirement he scored eighty-three using his left only.

At Jim's memorial service, the words of praise and condolences to Jim's family flooded in from PGA professionals such as Arnold Palmer, Ken Venturi, and Jack Nicklaus. Chris Thomas, Director of the Northern California PGA, stated, "His love for life, faith, family, and the game of golf was contagious. He will forever be remembered not only as a Pro's Pro, but also as an absolute gentleman." Casey Reamer, who worked with Jim, and the man chosen to succeed him, concluded, "Jim Langley was a man focused on his family, his members, his profession, and his faith, believing that his life had been a blessed journey. He was one of a kind. We've lost a lot."

I would like to express my gratitude to Jim Langley's Monterey Peninsula friends and neighbors who shared their stories and photographs of the man they admired so much. Bob Cushing, Frank LaRosa, Keith Crist, Casey Reamer, and Mrs. Louella Langley.

Photographs play a large role in an instruction book, so I must point out the artistry and care projected in the images captured by Jules Alexander, whose early career followed various sports but soon focused on Ben Hogan, as Jules recognized the "Mystique" of a true champion. Another artist is Walt Spitzmiller, art director for *Sports Illustrated* and *Golf Digest*, who provided the lovely painting of Ben Hogan for the end of this book.

Mike Lilly and his golfing family have shared their photos of masterful golfers from the modern era, at Tiger Woods' invitational tournament at Sherwood Oaks.

Ken West and Bill McLuckie created important images of Ben Hogan's swing.

Putting the book together in creative fashion was the task for Niels Aaboe, Senior Editor at Skyhorse Publishing, and for this attractive result I thank him and his colleagues.

My thanks to Darcy Dhillon, a main model who, as a young assistant professional at Point Grey, is headed for a happy career as a golf coach.

I am also indebted to Jeff Buder, head professional at Point Grey Golf Club. A serious golf competitor himself, he holds many insights into Ben Hogan's career, as well as the more fundamental swing needs of the keen amateur.

Friends like Des Dwyer, Gerry Kitson, Charles Hillman, Art Lilly, Percy Hoy, Dave Hurst, Paul Brown, Bob Mitchell, Greg Baydala, Paul Ormiston, Don Griffiths, Marie Donnici, Rose-Mary Basham, and Blair Thornton listened to my ramblings and questions with tolerance . . . and for that I am very grateful.

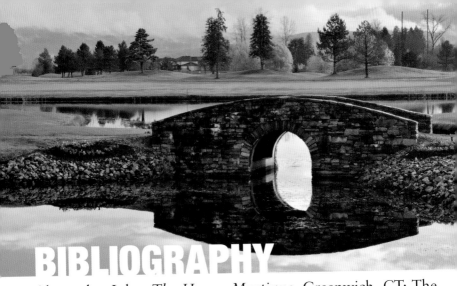

BIBLIOGRAPHY

Alexander, Jules. *The Hogan Mystique*. Greenwich, CT: The American Golfer Inc., 1994.

Andrisani, John. *The Hogan Way*. New York: HarperCollins, 2004.

Bertrand, Tom, and Printer Bowler. *The Secret of Hogan's Swing*. Hoboken: Wiley & Sons, 2006.

Dodson, James. *Ben Hogan: An American Life*. New York: Doubleday, 2004.

Farnsworth, Craig. *See It & Sink It*. New York: HarperCollins, 1997.

Frost, Mark. *The Match*. New York: Hyperion Books, 2007.

Hogan, Ben. *Ben Hogan's Five Lessons: The Modern Fundamentals of Golf*. New York: Simon and Schuster, 1957.

Hogan, Ben. *Power Golf*. New York: A.S. Barnes, 1948.

Hunt, Ted. *Ben Hogan's Magical Device: The Real Secret to Hogan's Swing Finally Revealed*. New York: Skyhorse, 2009.

Hunt, Ted. *Ben Hogan's Short Game Simplified*. New York: Skyhorse, 2010.

Nicklaus, Jack. *Golf My Way*. New York: Simon and Schuster Paperbacks, 1974.

Olson, Arv. *Backspin: 100 Years of Golf in British Columbia.* Vancouver: Heritage House, 1992.

Skyzinski, Rich. *The Quotable Hogan.* Nashville: Cumberland House, 2000.

Trevino, Lee. *The Snake in the Sandtrap.* New York: Holt, Rinehart and Winston. 1985.

Tschetter, Kris. *Mr. Hogan: The Man I Knew.* New York: Gotham Books, 2011.

Woods, Tiger. *How I Play Golf.* New York: Warner Books, 2001.

INDEX

Note: Entries to pictures are in *italics*.